Written by:
Doris Tanner Thomson

Dedicated to:
Donna Marie Tanner Shelden
Nina Dean Tanner Galland
Linda Louise Tanner Carothers
Martha Ilene Tanner Pulley
Mary Lois Tanner

A glimpse of a life lived in black and white. There may have been gray hues and some color, but in the years of the 1940's and 50's when the world seem less complicated, I remember it as serene with no drama and my recall is a sharp black and white.

The lines of right and wrong were plain, and there was no guessing where we stood. For the most part we would label it a peaceful time. There was a yearning however in each of us, for a world outside the land where our bare feet roamed; maybe somewhere beyond the horizon in another place not too far but just far enough we could return to the land.

Our young lives was during the era when the world was waking up from a depression which made our parents and grandparents, who lived it, more thankful for the blessings that came their way.

 This is our story from where I stood and as I remember it; a story of a man and his wife who forged a living off the land and successfully raised their daughters to appreciate what they had, and cherish their humble beginnings; a story of roots that run deep in the soil of the hill country of Tennessee.

THE WHIPPOORWILL'S SONG

By: Doris Thompson

March 2007 - 2014

Daddy

1908-2011

I've not always been fond of bag pipes. They give off a raspy sound of someone in pain regardless of what song they play. But there he was, the piper standing several feet away from the grave that was to receive my 102 year old father.

Regardless of how we anticipated the day, and regardless of how old a parent is, it is difficult to see them go. Life goes on but there is always a void which no one else can fill.

Since Mama died in February 1999, we knew this day would come. We knew there was long life in his family; we knew about his great grandpa Blankenship who had lived to be 110. We had seen his grave for our proof that someone in our ancestry had actually lived that long on this earth. We knew about his grandmother Blankenship who celebrated her 101st birthday before she died.

Daddy had determined he would live that long as well. He had no thoughts of dying. He was enjoying living and focused on getting to that ripe old age of 110. Grandma Tanner was 99 and her children for the most part had lived way into their 90's as well so for Daddy to strive to reach his ideal age was not as outrageous as it could appear.

"There is no one left on Long Branch I know anymore", he'd say in conversation. As he sat in the porch swing, with countless humming birds all round him; he reminisced about purchasing the land in the 1930's, paying Mr. Boyd a few dollars at a time and eventually getting the 150 acres paid off in short order. Taking a job in Michigan or wherever he could find work, he went wherever life took him, and made whatever sacrifice that confronted him, in order to realize the dream of owning his piece of the earth; where he would raise his family.

He had not lived a life of ease. Blood sweat and tears, as it were, still cry out on that farm and will forever be a reminder to future generations how hard he worked to reach the goal he had set. He had Mama, (Sarah Ellen Chapman) who worked equally as hard to help him realize the dream of raising his children to have more than he had, get a good education and not have to work as hard as women of his era had worked.

He had not planned any further than 12 years of schooling for his daughters. He had only gone to third grade himself; he had learn to read and write and do math necessary to keep from being cheated, or keep from cheating anyone.

The day of his home going, standing around his grave were his six daughters who were a success story he could talk about, stood with their families and extended families counting five generations.

Neighbors, friends and several generations each in their own thoughts about the man each of us knew as Father, Pawpaw, uncle, neighbor, Christian Brother, and so on.

As the piper was finishing his rendition of Amazing Grace, he walked slowly away from the funeral crowd until he could hardly be heard. Even though in the beginning it had (to me anyway) given out an eerie haunting sound, as the song came to a close the bagpipes again sounded out a forlorn almost lonely aura that slowly faded away, leaving the music echoing in our mind, and Amazing Grace wanting to roll of our tongue.

>Amazing Grace, How sweet the sound
>that saved a wretch like me
>I once was lost but now I'm found
>Twas blind but now I see.

The Christian Anthem we call it, for it tells of the Grace of a loving God who sent His son full of Grace and Glory to set us free from the penalty of Adams sin and more importantly our Sins.

Today as I write it is 2013. We stayed with him as long as we could. Daddy has made his trip to the other side, resting until Jesus comes to take the children of God away. Jesus power will break open the graves. Daddy's body will be changed in a "moment in the twinkling of an eye. It will be changed from grave clothes to clothes of righteousness, from mortal to immortal, and he will never taste/see death again." According to I Corinthians 15:51-57.

INTRODUCTION

Even though my life took me many places in this world of ours, my heart was never far from home. I did dream of leaving the farm one day, but at the time I didn't realize the impact of what that dream would have or how it would affect my life in later years. The farm was the green kingdom for the six girls who grew there. And though life has taken us each down a different path, somehow we've come back to appreciate our roots.

I understand now that staying around home is not a bad thing. Someone should carry on the family traditions. My family history has it, two of my great uncles walked out of the field where they had been plowing and never looked back. Where they wound up was several hundred miles from home. Evidently, the grass was greener in Alabama than on Long Branch, for they never returned.

Staying on the farm should have been my choice for I have longed to go back. Going back to the way things were is not possible, but maybe had I stayed, I would not have this yearning for the cornfields, the bottom lands or the woods where the animals were plentiful, the birds sang in chorus, and the Whippoorwill continued with his songs in the night.

Am I saying I'd like to be a little girl again? Well, isn't it true there is a child in all of us who yearns to come out and play? There is still a little girl in me which shows up occasionally. She is a prankster. She loves to laugh. She would love to skip rope, hang from the monkey bars, or chase the dog through the woods. She is a free spirit. Yet she loves solitude; solitude not to be selfish, but to dream. She dreams best when things are quiet. She dreams of tomorrow and she even has a plan as to how her tomorrows will turn out. Dreams which are different than when she was seven or even fourteen while strolling the new plowed fields or walking in the woods calling the cows while listening to the birds or looking for treasures.

The little girl which shows up occasionally helps me cope with the dreams I had of leaving the farm. Dreams I wish I had not had; dreams which came true the day after I graduated from High School when, with my sisters, I took the bus to Nashville to find work. I did not think of it as leaving, for I planned to come home on weekends and, in my reasoning, everything would remain the same. Mama and Daddy along with Linda, Martha and Lois would be where I left them and everything would stay the same. I could always come home and everything (everyone) would be in their place so my leaving did not have an impact on me. That is how I dreamed it at least. I could leave, but they would stay and remain the same.

Immature thinking to be sure; because somehow along the way those three little sisters grew up and came into womanhood and I wasn't even noticing. However, my happy-go-lucky self didn't think of consequences until it was too late. That is what I look back on.

For those who have moved away from a childhood home they will understand my thinking. Isn't this what happens at some point in our life, when the need to revisit home is strong?

Call it part of the aging process if you will, call it failing health, or whatever; the need to revisit yesterday comes very strongly at a point in our lives much more than when we were young with more future in front of us than past behind us. My recall comes and goes, so I've learned to pay attention when it does pull at my heartstrings. The urge is strongest when I hear a Whippoorwill call in the distance. And when I do I momentarily stop and go sit on the front porch in my reminiscence, where in an instant I remember another time and another place when things were simple – more black and white and I was carefree and full of wonder.

I think I've worked through the hard times. The times of deprivation, the lean times, or the times when we as children were punished in anger more severely than the crime we had committed called for. Looking now through adult eyes, one understands the frustrations of a mother of six growing girls. Sibling rivalry and bickering would cause any mother with more important things to do than listen to tattle tale girls to occasionally get frustrated.

It would be easy to have a well-trodden path back to the bad times, but God has helped when looking at those eras through adult eyes, to see things differently. It is easier to place oneself in the parent's shoes, knowing they were trying to provide in post-depression days. It is no wonder we may have been deprived of some basic necessities. The concentration was on surviving. And surviving meant food & shelter and clothes sufficient to keep us warm on cold days and modest on those hot summer days.

It is also easier now to see our parents were human, with feelings, with dreams and goals of their own. Happy? For the most part I think. However in going over my recalls, I can appreciate they were human subject to passions every other human has. They were Mama and Daddy to us, yet they were also male and female longing to be loved, appreciated and accepted.

I am not sure why I am dedicated with such passion to writing our story; a one sided story to be sure, for these few pages will be as I remember them. Others may add to these and our complete story will be told, but along with my memories will ultimately be a story of the man I call Daddy and my relationship with that man. A man I have learned to love and respect over the years, even if knowing him would have been much better. I have my memories, and his memories, which he has shared with us. As I write, I am past 70 years old, and am at a vantage point in my own life where surely I can be objective in my observations. Each of us is a product of many people who have had influence into molding and shaping our lives. Beginning with parents, and grandparents we are many people combined into one person. So it is with that in mind, I will attempt to show you the man, the husband, the father, the brother and neighbor; I will endeavor to stand outside myself and see him as others saw him.

    As for Mama, she will not be left out. She was very much a part of life on the farm. Often I see her more so than I do Daddy when my pondering takes me back. She was always there whereas Daddy was busy with what farmers do who have a family. He was eking out a living on a farm with much new ground which was needed for grazing pastureland. Mama was always close by. Home was where we found her. She was home. Regardless of where we were, we felt at home if Mama was there.

    Life is what we make it I'm told. We are who we are. We were planned from the beginning of time and God says, "He knew us" before we were formed in the womb. He remembers our frame - He knows our down sittings and our uprisings and our thoughts before we think them. There is nothing private I guess. Psalms 139)

    In each life there is a story the world may want to hear. It seems to give significance in having a story to tell, whether good or bad it proves we've lived. Just writing it down for future generations will serve as history as well.

    For I pray there will also be a time when my children and their children and on to more generations will also want to know something about life on that piece of land that runs deep in my soul; with my blood sill flowing in their veins so deep that they too can feel a part of that land for years to come when they drive through Tennessee and decide to go by the place of my birth and stay until evening where they can listen closely for the Whippoorwill song.

CHAPTER 1

"Doris!" Mother called from the kitchen door. I was not ready to answer and I was out of sight, so I waited for her to call again. I had learned I could keep doing what I was doing, which was akin to nothing, before she got serious and called again.

"Doris!" she called a little louder. Still I did not budge.

"Doris Ann!" Adding my middle name meant she was getting serious. She never used my middle name unless she was in earnest about her reason to call, so I decided it was time to answer.

"What?" I answered knowing it was the wrong thing to say.

"What did you say young lady?" she yelled. Answering "what" to my parents was punishable by whatever means she was in the mood for.

"Sorry I meant, Ma'am!" I answered politely.

"Come take this jug of water to your daddy. He needs a fresh drink so hurry."

I left my project and moved at my own pace to the kitchen where she was busy at her particular projects.

"Do you know which field he is in?"

"No ma'am!"

She handed me the fresh jug of cold water and said, "In the field behind the house pass the peanut patch. Hurry and try not to spill any."

I did as she instructed. I took the water jug trying not to slosh any out as I hurried across the newly furrowed ground, my beloved dog Jack at my heels. I loved the feel of the warm soil under my bare feet. I headed in the general direction of the field, my cotton dress flapping around my legs, and listened for Daddy's call to the team of mules as he guided the plow across the field. Between commands to the mules, he whistled. I could tell he was lost in his work when he was whistling. His whistling made me know all was going well that day.

Then, I saw him walking behind the plow – silhouetted against the brown mules in front of him and the row of lush green trees and brush which divided the fields beyond him. Brown from days of working in the sun, he was a sturdy man of six feet tall. His hazel eyes focused on his work. They were eyes that never really looked at me. I wanted them to, but he had a way of looking past and beyond me instead.

His features were regular I guess. His hazel eyes and a mouth which showed few smiles accented his bronzed face. To me, his hands were large and calloused from gripping the well-worn handle of the aging plow.

I waited for him to get to the end of the row and start back toward me. I lifted my hand in a wave to get his attention. He looked up from the plowing to see me. "Whoa, Whoa" he called to the team. He may have said something like "Brought me a drink of water did ye?"

I lifted the jug up to his waiting hands and stood there kicking the dirt as he drank. Shortly bringing the jug away from his mouth, he wiped his chin then raised his well-worn sweat drenched hat to cover his eyes. Judging the time of day, he looked toward the sky with squinted eyes. I did not understand how he could tell time by the sun but it was something for which he was good.

He finished drinking the water, then handed me the empty jug, wiped the water from his chin and said, "My, that was a fine drink of water". I took that as a "Thank you" and without further exchange of words, he called the team to attention and they continued pulling the plow across the field.

He was a man of few words so I did not expect anything more than what he said. Probably would not have known how to reply had he made conversation. I knew when he was angry. Anger brought our attention to him. Mama was our buffer, and though Daddy supplied our needs monetarily, we received everything we had need of from her hands.

I started toward home never looking back,

I had finished my task. Playing as I went, and feeling the warm soil under my bare feet, I took my time, I sang as I walked stopping occasionally to teach the chickens whatever was on my mind. I had been going to school for one year, and was eager to pass on anything I had learned.

I did not know much, but my students were none the wiser. Jack, our faithful Shepherd Collie walked when I walked, and as I stopped to make a point in my "lesson" Jack stopped. He perked up his ears, turned his head up then down seemingly in agreement. As I continued my walking and talking, he kept up with me. Often he ran ahead, stopped and waited for me to catch up wagging his tail in anticipation of my next move. I was in no particular hurry for I figured Mama would have another errand for me, and I was sure it would not fit into my plans.

I looked up toward the farmhouse in the distance. Mama was busy feeding the chickens. She was every bit five feet four inches tall, wore her long dark hair in a bun. The weight she had gained from having children had stayed glued to her body. I never noticed her size. A child doesn't. She was Mama. She concentrated on the job at hand, shy where strangers were concerned; she was talkative but could also be the quiet sort, saying only what she had to say in the course of her day. Until of course, she was riled and then everyone knew.

Three-year-old Linda was usually close by. She had to be wherever Mama was. With four girls and a farmer to care for, Mama found no time to have an afternoon siesta. There was little rest for women of her era who were married to men of the field. Her responsibilities of making a home for her family with few amenities didn't help as electricity had not found its way to the rural country of Tennessee, and would not for several more years.

I caught the scent of food coming from the kitchen in the Shanty. It had to be white northern beans with a salty piece of fatback. The smell drifted through the air to my nose, tantalizing my appetite. Oh my, I wondered if I could wait 'til supper time to taste Mamas friend chicken, fried potatoes and northern beans. The whiff caused my steps to quicken almost to a trot in my hurry to get home. Mama and Linda were feeding the chickens so they did not notice me as I passed. I took myself through the back door where I would pass the wood stove in the kitchen.

"Yep, beans like I thought" I said as I peeked into each pot taking a deep breath of its contents. "Yippee" I yelled after I opened the skillet with fried chicken. Going into the front room where Donna and Dean were. Dean asked, "What was that all about?"

My answer came quickly, "beans and chicken for supper!" Donna was eleven and Dean would soon be nine.

They were of the age to be Mama's helpers. I am sure Donna had learned to cook and in retrospect, I believe Dean was cooking also and for sure us all washed dishes. It seemed it was my job to run errands. I think I could accomplish more on the outside of the kitchen. I got in their way! Eating was on my agenda, but cooking, well I am still learning today.

We knew our chores. So without being told, we each took a pail or jug with a handle, and walked to the spring for fresh water. Like children on a mission, we marched across the gravel road, and then down a small rocky grade that turned right across a root, which conveniently placed, gave us a place to step. We kept our footing as we walked the rocky slope a few more steps before turning left. The path was in the shape of the letter S, curving around roots and taking the path of least resistance. At the end of the path was our destination, a spring with cool water, clear as crystal flowed from under the bluff.

"Bring back a gallon of milk for supper" Mama had called as we were leaving. The bluff had an overhang, and under it, Daddy had built a fence around the protruding bluff so milk and butter would be safe from pests as the spring branch served as our refrigerator.

Donna opened the gate, retrieved the milk, and then we each dipped our pail into the water for our journey back up the hill. I do not remember when the first time I had taken my place with the evening chores. It seemed I always had. My legs had strengthened and the climb up was easy. We had so often done the chore of bringing water to the house, it had become boring. Therefore, on each trip I made alone, I made up games. I tried to see how far I could count from the road to the spring. Or I tried not to spill even a drop on my way back up. Sometimes I stopped in the bend of the curve, walked out on the ledge of another bluff to look out over the world beyond. No one was the wiser of my attempt of challenging the boredom. But it worked for me.

Inside the house, we poured our water into a bigger container, saving some for drinking water. The wood cook stove had a reservoir built into the right side where water was kept warm and served for cooking as well.

"Mama, I hear daddy coming in from the field!" I yelled as though Mama was at a neighbor's house two farms up the road.

"You don't have to yell. I see him," mama quipped as she came through the kitchen door.

Daddy had judged his time well from looking at the sun, so around 5:30 on the late May afternoon, he and the team of mules walked home. I watched from the fence as he removed their harness and turned them loose to run. He took the pitchfork loaded with hay and threw it into their stall, whistling as he did. When he finished I walked home with him. It was just good to be walking with him. I wanted to hold his hand, but I didn't dare reach up to grasp it and with all my clattering about anything and nothing, he showed no signs of acknowledgement that I was there.

    Mama's tasks were finished and she was back in the house when he came in. Dean had gathered the eggs. Hence, as far as I was concerned we were ready to eat. Donna had set the table; we knew where we were supposed to set. Each one had an assigned chair and not once did we deviate from one meal to another. I know Mama seemed conscious about thanking the Lord for our blessing of food, so someone prayed, not sure who as Daddy didn't start until later
    There was some conversation while we ate, but mostly we enjoyed the bounty set before us. Such was a day in the life of our family.

CHAPTER 2

From the year 2007 I began writing our story as I remember it. Daddy is still living at this time. Born in the year of 1908, he has witnessed many changes in his 99 -year life span. At this point he has outlived his family and very few people of his era still live to tell the story of their early days together. Tennessee has him listed among the centenarians who live in the state.

I understand the number of men and women who live to be one hundred plus in years is growing each year. For him to have had a good mind even to this end is phenomenal. Except for his hearing loss, he is very vocal and for the most part his memories are still sharp and vivid.

He wants to share about his life. His memory is sharp and it seems to center on the good parts of his life. It seems he has left the bad times and memories in their place. In the past; which is a good lesson for us all I'd say. When ask about his long years, he says: "It doesn't seem like 99 years. Life went so fast."

That is truly something to take home with anyone and eat on it for a while. As we live in such a rush rush world in the 21st century not knowing what tomorrow will bring, we hear a man who has lived many more years than we can even imagine living say, "It went by so fast."

Farming was Daddy's trade. He was the

first in his family to purchase land. His dad had been a sharecropper never able to get enough money ahead to purchase any property to call his own.

From his early years, Dad was a driven man with an insatiable desire to own his piece of the earth. In 1927, shortly after becoming a young man of eighteen he connected with some local men who were going to Michigan in search of their fortune or future at least. He started working in the factories soon after he arrived, making automobile parts. As the custom was in those days of no Hotels, he lived in a boarding, or as some historians say, a rooming house, and soon Clyde and Romie, two of his brothers, came to try their luck at factory work. He had no trouble saving money, and even with the factories not paying much he managed to pay his bills and save a tidy sum.

America for the most part was coming alive. The era called the roaring 20's had more people living in the cities than left to farm the land. It was also known as a time of prosperity and wealth. It was a time of Peace as well. The automobile was becoming more popular. The new technologies had brought the voice of the world inside the homes of those who owned a radio.

World War I had lasted from 1914 - 1919 and bloody war though it was with many men losing their life, the United States was coming back from the devastation and its citizens were enjoying prosperity and Peace.

However no one could predict what a few years down the road would hold for anyone.

The Stock Market crash in 1929 caused a layoff of most workers. Therefore, Daddy and his brothers were among the first to receive their layoff notice. With layoff notices in hand, they pooled their money and bought a car to go back home to Tennessee.

The stock market crash affected everyone without prejudice. It took a while for the impact of the crash to sink in. The banks had invested their deposits in the stock market, with high hopes the economy would stay on the ultimate high. With the stock market tumbling, the banks then closed their doors. They had no money in which to give back to those who had entrusted to them their life's savings.

The Stock Market crash however, had made poor men out of millionaires, and around every corner the homeless looked through garbage cans for a bite to eat. Mass poverty occurred when the great depression set in. People were forced to live in shantytowns, and it is reported that at least one third of Americans were below the poverty level.

In the community of Long Branch as well as the communities around, men had returned from Michigan to work at anything that would help buy a bag of beans. Reports were that one out of four Americans could not find jobs. As Daddy had gone to Detroit in 1927 when he was only 18 and immediately found work and a place in which to sleep, it was short lived.

Upon returning home, he sold his part in the car they had purchased to one of his brothers. He could hold onto money anyway; to have a dollar meant more to him than a car.

The deadly grip of the depression held on for years. Until the presidential elections in 1933 when Franklin Roosevelt took office, the banking system ceased to function. He closed all the banks in America for a three-day holiday. Some banks were than cautiously opened with regulations on limited withdrawals. FDR responded to the Great Depression by creating a New Deal to restore the nation's confidence. The New Deal consisted of 3 R's: Relief, Recovery and Reform. The Relief was to help the unemployed and poor, the Recovery was for the economy to return to normal levels and the Reform was to prevent the financial system from going back into a repeat depression.

Roosevelt though Republican by party, ran as an independent. He had an eye on the future, and seeing things turning around, devised a program to put men to work. Mostly on projects that required manual labor. With Uncle Sam meeting the payroll, countless bridges, highways and parks were constructed including the Hoover Dam which was built between 1931 and 1936 during the great depression.

Daddy however continued to work the land with his father, and if he took advantage of the WPA (**Work Projects Administration**: the former federal agency (1935–43) charged with instituting and administering public works in order to relieve national unemployment), I am not sure. It is reported that some eight point 5 million people went to work for the WPA. Regardless of location, whether city or farm, whether adult or child, the difficult times effected everyone.

He lived with his parents during those hard times.

"Arthur, I hear they are hiring back at the factory", Romie came by to report one afternoon. His excitement led to Daddy's going back to Michigan to work a while more.

By the time he returned home the next time to Tennessee in he was 24. He had caught a ride home numerous other times but this visit was different. He had not yet married and coming back to his roots, he was ready to settle down.

By nature, he was very shy. To initiate a conversation was rare for him. It did not help that the crop of girls available were not to his liking. Barn dances, church pie suppers and socials brought people out from neighboring farms for recreation, families that may never have left their home otherwise. When rumors of a social were generated, families hitched their team of mules to their wagon and went whatever distance to be there. Others carried their food contribution, walking the distance.

Picnics on the ground were of no help either as after awhile the same girls came to each gathering and none of them was what he was looking for.

He picked up odd jobs and helped his Dad and Brothers farm. Being a sharecropper was not what he wanted to do the rest of his life. He wanted land of his own. He had a hunger for land that started in his youth. The dream was on his mind and in his vision, until there would be no rest until his dream was realized. It kept pounding its way into his head with every heartbeat.

In late summer, the Chapman brothers were in a brush arbor revival meeting in the community. It was not something he would do normally, but being a young man, he figured that surely he could find some girls there. The evangelist had a sister who had come to visit the revival that night. Daddy scanned the crowd - did not see anyone worth taking home to mama, and took his place in the back of the brush arbor.

Sometimes during the evening, he saw a young girl he had not seen on his initial inventory of the crowd and his heart did a flip-flop as he declared, "That is my girl, if I never get her".

"He was a catch," Mama alleged. "All the girls wanted him." We giggled as she told us her side of the story never taking our eyes off her. As little girls will, we were female enough to wonder if when our time came for a husband our story would be similar.

"My Daddy, thought he was a no good drifter. Unstable was the word he used. Since he had many jobs, he wasn't sure if he could support a family."

Their actual courting days were few as the distance between them meant getting to see each other when he could catch a freight train to Paris, from Tennessee Ridge.

"I become a hobo, sneaking rides on the old coal train cars, jumping off close to her house just to see her." He loved to tell us. "Nearly broke my arm once, jumping off that moving train."

Such courting conditions made it difficult for her Father (Logan Chapman) to get acquainted with him. Eventually Granddad Chapman reluctantly gave Daddy permission to marry his daughter, after two years of a long distance relationship.

They met when Mother was 15. On March 27, 1934, they started their life together. Daddy would soon be 26 and Mama had turned 17 the month before. Waiting two years was no problem to speak of. As it stood seventeen was still young for marrying even in 1934 but it was a common occurrence.

Somehow, he had not planned their immediate future very well to say the least. Where he was going to take his new wife had evidently not occurred to him. Therefore, on their wedding night, he took his young bride to his mother and fathers house.

The house was built with a breezeway down the middle of two separate sections; living quarters and sleeping quarters on both sides of the breezeway. The breezeway served as a porch, or a place for entertaining under the dry of the roof that joined the two sections. Many homes in the twenties and thirties had been built on this fashion.

"We went to his mother and Dad's house for our wedding night" Mama stated in a matter of fact tone. Her tone suggested she had accepted it to be what it was and there was no need being sour about it now.

"I didn't like the idea, but I was too young to protest, and in those days you did what your husband said regardless. It didn't make for a good relationship between his mother and me. I never did think she liked me. I think she tolerated me but there was always something that wasn't quite right about our relationship. It was strained at best. Oh we stayed cordial. Maybe it was the Mother-in-law stigma that has been around for hundreds of years. I don't know."

She continued talking in a reminiscent way; her mind going from one thing to another. "No honeymoon, just the neighborhood chivalry on the night we got married."

A young bride with no privacy had to be devastating, I thought, *with her being so young and innocent and hardly ready for married life the way it started out.*

However, if love had anything to do with it, she would have followed him anywhere. He adored her and she him.

It wasn't long until he found a little house in Whippoorwill Hollow. He had bought a couple beds when he was working, so at least they had a bed and a mattress of feathers. Someone gave them a stove and table, so they were good to go. It was not the Holiday Inn, but it was home. Mama spent the pregnancy with her first baby in the unsightly place where newspapers lined the walls.

"I was so very sick and was for most of the pregnancy." She had arrived to a point in her story to continue.

"Mama came to visit but she still had Louise at home. It was hard for them to get away much, but Mama and Louise came as much as they could."

As it stood, Mother was alone most days as any hope of neighbors was despairing for the miles which separated them.

"The pictures on the wallpaper seem to laugh at me and my situation," she confessed once. In her trauma of pain and loneliness, she said the pictures of people on the news papered walls seemed to come off the page tormenting and laughing at her dilemma. It was not a good time to look back on. So as it was she said very little more about it.

"I thought I was going crazy," she said. However, her new baby brought joy to what she led me to believe about her otherwise dismal life. Donna Marie was born in Whippoorwill Hollow on July 12 1936, during one of the hottest summers in the history of Tennessee with one Tennessee city recording 110 degrees. I can only add *how terrible it must have been on her, even though the house being in the shade of the hollow may have brought some relief from the intense heat.* She was still very young to have had her first baby and to feel so alone.

By the time Donna came, Daddy had made up his mind that going back to Michigan was the only answer if he was ever to make a living and realize the dream of owning his peace of the earth.

Some time passed before he began looking for a more suitable place for his little family but a house on Lewis Branch came available so he moved their few belongings there.

"Sarah, we have got to go to Michigan."

Daddy announced to her as though they had already had a former conversation. Mama was in the 7th month of her second pregnancy.

"What did you say?" she asked with a lack of enthusiasm. She moved around about the room trying to find a place to rest.

"Everybody else is going up north to work in the factories." He responded as if he were still trying to say the words out loud. He had the words on his mind for several months and was processing them through his brain, and now he had let them come pass his lips.

"I talked to Mr. Alonzo Boyd about that ninety three acres on Long Branch next to Irvin Tomlinson place. Has some good rich bottom land and good grazing ground for cattle." He continued as she sat trying to listen. "Good place for a garden too", he added as an after thought.

He paused before he continued. "If we move back to Detroit", he finally said "when you git able to travel, we would be able to pay off the land in a few years"

The subject was then dropped for a few months. Mama was concentrating on having another baby. Nina Dean was born on November 19, 1938 and still the move had not happened. Every waking minute of his day, he worked on the details of his plan. Though it was not something he admitted, land would give him a sense of self worth. Winter was no time to start north since the snows were bad. It just gave him a longer time to plan their move.

CHAPTER 3

Also 1938 in Europe, Germany was continuing its strategy of persecuting the Jews. German troops invaded Austria, and later Poland, making World War II a sure sign of the times to stop the aggression of Adolf Hitler.

Nineteen Thirty eight, followed a number of years of success with the US economy. Then a recession hit which caused unemployment to rise again to 19%. Eventually the minimum hourly wage was 40 cents per hour for a 44 hour working week.

It seemed that again there was no one left untouched by the troubled times.

German Nazis launched a campaign of terror against Jewish people, their homes and businesses in Germany and Austria leaving at least 100 dead and over 30,000 arrested and sent to concentration camps. *(The peoples History Blog, 1938 News and tidbits from History.)*

Daddy's strategy however was formed, mostly in his mind, and soon would come time to put them into action. Going to Detroit was the only solution he could see. He would be able to find work. The US was gearing up for the impending war and factories were making parts for the Military. They needed all the help they could get.

The great drought of the 30's had kept farmers paralyzed, but some had no other recourse but to farm. Though the great dustbowl was more out west, Tennessee was not exempt from its fury. When the dryness, heat and grasshoppers destroyed the crops, farmers were left with no money to buy groceries or make a farm payment. The frantic feeling of what was to come, and what they saw as the dismal future ahead caused many to walk away from their farms and migrate to the west. Their farms being in foreclosure caused a hopelessness that left them drained and weary from trying against the odds.

The government offer commodities or some would say care packages, or otherwise many would have had nothing to feed their families.

Everyone was going to Michigan or Ohio, and "if I am going to buy the land, I got to take the plunge." He said thoughtfully. Eventually, the decision for a moving day came. He and mother with their two little girls' ages two and six months were on their way. His handshake and a hundred dollars down payment to Mr. Boyd had sealed the deal and the land was almost his. As it was, the Boyd farm had passed hands many times already, and it always went back to Mr. Boyd due to non-payments. In telling the story to us he smiled and said, "Alonzo thought he would get it back from me too, but I was determined it was mine."

His brother Clyde along with his family lived in the shanty on the land, farming and tending to the cattle Daddy had managed to purchase. A few yearlings were a good start he decided.

At last in Michigan Mother had what she considered was a nice house with furniture and running water, it should have been enough for her to be happy. And for the most part she was. She had her babies, was living in a big city and each day could have been a venture, but it was lost in her loneliness. She had never lived outside of Tennessee or very far from her family and she had some adjusting to do.

Her home was an apartment, a portion of a house that had been divided into sections. It was of a good size to house boarders; other men who had come north to work, leaving their families behind. Daddy worked in the factory and together they had one purpose - to one day go back to Tennessee and live off the land.

"When I git the farm I will be able to make a living." He had said to encourage Mother. So with their hearts in agreement they worked toward their goal.

Mama was so proud of her home. The relationship between her and Daddy was not to her liking, in fact very difficult. However women in the late 30's and early 40's had no alternative but to stay the course and hope for the best. Some may have chosen to walk away from their marriage vows, but that was not her upbringing. She complied with his wishes the best she could while crying in secret and praying in the closet.

Her children were safe, they had a place to play, and she found the park and took them on picnics. Days filled with washing babies or clothes, cooking or washing dishes, she found herself missing and needing her mother and the family. For someone who was raised in a large household of four girls and four boys, moving to Michigan was like being on the other side of the world. Letter writing was doable but she needed more.

She was still in her twenties and young enough to need her family especially her mother for guidance and help in raising her girls. I maintain that the Lord always provides our needs; in fact His Word declares that He will. Php 4:19 "But my God shall supply all your need according to his riches in glory by Christ Jesus." In looking back, I see His plan unfolding for Mama.

The wash area was in the basement of the old two-story house.

"Hello. I've seen you here before doing your wash, my name is Mildred Crumbaker" the elderly woman introduced herself.

"My name is Sarah Tanner and we just moved here about a month ago. Do you live around here?" Mama asked shyly.

Mrs. Crumbaker was older than Mama who lived next door and needed someone to mother. As Mama was shy in some ways for sure, and having never lived in a big city before, people she met were strangers. To see her and Mrs. Crumbaker visiting and working together leaves much to my imagination. It was an accidental meeting definitely, but one that was meant to be. Mother and Mrs. Crumbaker shared every spare minute together, sharing cooking ideas and tending to small children as well as her own preteens. Mrs. Crumbaker became the dearest friend Mama had during her years there.

Soon the signs of morning sickness let her know that another baby was on the way.

"Oh God, help me" she prayed. "I have two little ones and I don't want to go through another pregnancy.

She had been pregnant all her married life, or that was her feelings anyway. "I wish I could talk to Mama," she wailed into her apron after she vomited again.

"I'm so tired of waiting on everybody. Arthur, these men who eat at my table, all of them can't do nothing for themselves. Everybody depends on me."

She continued pouring out the pitiful sounds of a breaking soul in between heaving into the commode. As she raised her head and wiped her face with her apron, she continued her out burst. Hormonal, and weary of life the way it was, she sobbed until she fell quiet.

"What's wrong Mama," soon to be four-year-old Donna asked as she walked into the bathroom.

"You sick?"

"I'll be alright hon; I'm just having a bad time right now." She tried to console her young daughter. Mama got up washed the tears away and finished her day. Distraught, queasy and tired, she finished the supper meal for the boarders and Daddy in spite of her desire to just go somewhere and lay down.

It was I this time, Doris Ann, born in 1940, on June 9, 19 months after Nina Dean. They had made the trip back to Tennessee while Mama was still able to travel. It was there her mother with the help of the local Doctor could deliver the baby as they had the other two.

"I had went back to Michigan and left her for Mama and Papa to watch after" Daddy said. "I got back a few days after Doris was born. Your mama was still in the bed. I reached for Dean who was the baby when I left them a few months earlier, but your Mama misunderstood. She thought I should have reached for the new baby. I just didn't think."

I suffered from low self-esteem for many years due to the story I heard which went like this: When you were born, your Daddy didn't even look at you. He was disappointed you weren't a boy.

It was good to hear his confession and so simple it was - it made sense. He may not have been excited about three girls, but he was a man who took care of his family. In those days men may not have known exactly how to treat their wife, and maybe Mama needed more but again in retrospect he did what he could with what he knew. And so be it if God was going to give him a house full of girls, one doesn't question God's choice.

After I was born and Mother was able to travel again Daddy took his growing family and returned to Michigan to finish paying for the farm.

I'm sure his job was rewarding, in that he was making a living at last and life was good. He had sent money to Mr. Boyd continuing to pay for the land but he knew the time would come when going back to Tennessee to make his home was inevitable.

It is amazing what comes as the earliest memories for me. Cloudy recollections, of a promise from my grandfather, that "if you'll walk with me all the way to the corner, I'll buy you a sucker."

As some children who do not walk until they are over 12 months old, I remember doing just that. The corner could not have been very far, and he came through with his promise. For Granddaddy Chapman to have been there makes me know he had not come alone. Though I don't remember I'm sure Grandmamma Chapman had come as well.

Living so close to the street made it difficult for Mother to keep the neighborhood children away from Donna and Dean. Somehow, neither she nor Daddy trusted anyone they didn't know. Call it a hill country malady, or then again, maybe there were reasons to be afraid; for they lived in a minority neighborhood of people from other countries, mostly Poland. The word Daddy used was "Pollock's" to describe those of Polish descent.

Donna had heard his rant about someone he had worked with getting, as he thought, preferential treatment. She had only picked up part of the word and used it one day in an argument which pursued. "You little whop," Was all she could get out of her mouth when she jumped in to defend her territory.

"The city is no place to raise girls," Daddy said after he heard about the "fight".

It had taken him most of three years to save what he would need to purchase a mule for plowing and equipment for harvesting However the deciding factor on the time to move back to Long Branch came when he realized that the streets of Detroit was no place to raise girls. As a result moving day came.

It was in the fall of 1943, I guess it was about the second thing I remember, and then only partially. I was a few months passed three years old. Moving must have been a big ordeal, for I remember Mama packing and helping us to understand there was going to be big changes to take place in our lives. I only remember as far as getting into the automobile, and then I must have gone back to sleep for a few years.

CHAPTER 4

We weren't back In Tennessee but about eight months when we were sent to the O'Guins home. I remember very little as I was only four and paying attention to my surroundings was not part of my make-up anyway. I lived in my own world.

The O'Guins was a home of two women, Miss Lil and Hinnon, a mother and daughter, and the mother's brother Bass who lived on a farm adjoining ours. It was a good place to stay during birthing time at home. Mama was in labor with Linda Louise who was so tiny at birth, the Doctor said she was a preemie and very delicate. July 25, 1944 brought yet another girl, making our female number of 5 including Mama.

Being four I sure didn't pay much attention to a sister being a mere baby myself. It didn't take long however for me to warm up to the baby; she was someone to play with as well as mimic me, making me laugh.

Dad's brother Clyde and his family lived on the Irvin Tomlinson farm, helping Mr. Tomlinson do the yearly crops. Occasionally we'd walk the mile to see them. After a visit we'd start home in time to do the chores. One day on our trip home, we heard a car coming, and we all got in a line behind each other to allow the car room to pass. I had felt as big as any of them in our family, so I proceeded to pick Linda up (who was the youngest) and growing up too fast. And even though I was taller than she, I picked her up anyway. I struggled at carrying her in my arms, until the car was in sight and I set her down and left her standing there. I didn't have forethought about the danger I was leaving her in. until Mama looked back and saw Linda standing a few yards behind us and a car approaching. You talk about learning a lesson - Mama had a way of making a lesson adhere my pea brain. Sorry Linda!!

Between 1940 and 1944, Mama had a miscarriage. It seemed she just couldn't carry boy babies to term. Again in the years following 1944, she had another miscarriage which was again a boy. It would have been nice to have had brothers, I think. Often I feel we missed out on something by not growing up with a brother. Then again, we made such good memories as sisters without having the experience I won't even bother letting my imagination go there. God plans our ways, and places us in the families He has fore chosen. He chooses our heritage, and from the foundation of the world, He knew our lifespan. From the first breath to the last - He has seen it with the sweep of His eyes. We are so fortunate to know He has us on His mind. Oh how I want to follow His plan and not miss out on what He has planned for our family.

Jeremiah 29:11 *For I know the thoughts that I think toward you, saith Jehovah, thoughts of peace, and not of evil, to give you hope in your latter end.*
Jeremiah 29:12 *And ye shall call upon me, and ye shall go and pray unto me, and I will hearken unto you.*

Jeremiah 29:13 *And ye shall seek me, and find me, when ye shall search for me with all your heart.*

CHAPTER 5

At seven, I had not been informed of where babies came from. I paid no attention to Mama's swelling belly or her weight gain. I, for sure, never noticed that she was tired or that she moved about more slowly than at her usual steady pace. Unlike Daddy who passed his time whistling, she was quiet unless we had riled her about something. From all the demands of a growing family, there were days when her endurance was threadbare, and we had learned to scurry out of her path.

She was a dreamer. She loved Daddy but there was something missing. Most marriages have trouble in spite of promising before "God and these witnesses" to hang in there for better or worse. For the most part their marriage was on the better side, but other times it was on the dark side of worse we learned in later years. Often she could walk away or close her ears and pretend the demands on her life were not there. Then on other days, dreaming helped her finish her day without crying. Dreams of another life where there would be no responsibilities and respect was easier to come by or start all over drawing her line in the sand before the gulf between them got this big, maybe be the little girl again, where her dreams could end as she wanted them to.

The dreaming was short lived, for the mother's heart that beat in her chest caused her to look on the faces of her children and immediately know that to have 4 little girls and another baby on the way was the best thing in life to her. Then she would tuck the dream away in her heart for another day when she needed an escape.

Having married Daddy when she was 17, she admitted, "Just a child. I was just a child!" Daddy was a man of the world in comparison, being twenty-six, had done some traveling, plus working out of state. "He was a catch, all the girls envied me," she added.

"I went from Daddy's house to my husband's house," she said on one of her dreaming days. Truly, there was no stop in between. The duties at her mothers' house were to clean up after all her brothers. Her duties at the home she made with her husband stayed the same in so many ways. She was still cleaning, but this time after a farmer who did nothing to help himself when it came to making her job a little easier.

She was born and raised in the Henry County of Paris, Tennessee in 1917 to Logan and Addie Hodges Chapman. With four brothers and three sisters, she was next to Louise who was the youngest. In the beginning, she was able to take the teasing her brothers dished out. Her older sisters who cared deeply for her cushioned the brothers' attempts at fun. The good beginnings stopped however, when she was nine.

It was 1947 and she was adding another baby to her already overloaded life. Bare foot and pregnant was the slogan for the forties and fifties. She was fertile and the babies kept coming.

She had finished canning and preserving the vegetables from the garden. Invoking the help of Donna, Dean and myself, she gave each of us a container and instructed us on how to pick pole beans.

"Be careful not to pull so hard you destroy the vine. They are still producing beans," she instructed.

I do not know how I managed to be the one that did something wrong, but I was forever getting into trouble. Somehow, I had a world going on in my head where I was Queen and everyone else my royal subjects. I had my own set of rules and mine were mixed up with those Mama had lain out. I could not seem to remember hers. I do not remember if the vines survived another picking.

In the evening we sat around the living room stringing beans. The only talking was between us girls. Mostly me, I always had something to say. Daddy gave me the eye now and then which told me to shut up awhile. I kept quiet, until another thought made its way to my active mind, and invariably what I said sometimes brought a laugh.

"Oh! Ah-oh" Mama wincing in pain, holding her stomach and a look of concerned crossed her face. She and Daddy exchanged some words in code that we understood only years later.

"You girls get ready for bed now, we'll finish these beans in the morning", she suddenly lost the urgency of getting the beans done. We got up and got ourselves ready for bed.

Morning came, and Mama could not get out of bed to prepare our breakfast. Daddy did his specialty of left over biscuits and fresh gravy so we would have something to sustain us for the day.

"You kids stay outside today and play. Aunt Nora is coming to help your mama. She ain't feeling good today."

It was not an unusual request but hearing Mama moaning in the other room we left our plates on the table and went to play.

After her miscarriages, Mama's body was weary from having babies with no rest period in between. In addition, with each pregnancy, her health deteriorated. She had given birth to Linda in July after returning to Long Branch from Michigan.

So it was in August 1947 the mid wives, Miss Lill, Hennon, Aunt Nora and possibly Grandma Tanner came to the house to help with the delivery of the baby and have things ready for the Doctor when he came. Daddy had let the women know the labor had started. He had summoned the Doctor, so he would arrive later. With everything taken care of, he went about his work leaving the women stuff to his sister-in-law, mother and the neighbors.

Aunt Nora being a mother of three brought her children to play with us while she was busy. Donald, Orman and Evonne were good for us. More like brothers and another sister than first cousins. Donna and Dean were to watch three year old Linda, but we all watched after each other really. Evonne was only two years older than Linda, and two years younger than me. Orman and I were the same age, and Donald and Donna were the oldest.

We had been playing awhile when we heard the crushing of gravel in the distance. The sound was a distinct one, for there were not many people who owned cars even in 1947. Sure enough from around the curve coming from town, a black car sped down the dirt road and stopped in front of our house. Shortly Dr. Atkins stepped out of the car, his black bag in hand, hurried up the steps and bounded into the house in a flash without any acknowledgement of the children who stood and watched his every move.

Donald concluded that each time the Doctor came; he left a baby that had not been there before. And, he always left girls!

Sure enough, a baby cried shortly after the Doctor disappeared into the house. Donald's face lit up with excitement.

"The next time that Doctor comes with that black bag, I'm going to trip him", he said with the flare of a Politician. He, being the oldest of the seven of us, made us take notice of his intelligence that maybe he had hit upon a truth. The truth being, that "surely the Doctor had a baby in that black bag and he moved passed us without us hearing its cries".

Aunt Nora came out on the porch to announce we had another baby sister. Donald proudly told his mother his plan concerning the Doctor. "I think that might be a good idea", she laughed as she went back into the house.

The mid wives stayed around after Martha was born, and the Doctor had left orders that Mama stay in bed. All Mamas' deliveries had been difficult. Her body had hardly time to rest when she was pregnant again. Bed rest was what she needed for sure. The friends who served as midwives had arranged to come for several days afterwards to serve Mama and see we were fed.

We learned Mama had named the new baby girl Martha Ilene; how much she weighed was probably important to the adults but to us it didn't matter. The day was August 21, 1947; another hot day with temperatures pushing 100 degrees.

We were introduced to the little sister, but being so young, we went on about our business in short fashion. It was nothing new to me being a seven year old; I had experienced it three years earlier when Linda was born. Martha Ilene was a pretty baby. All the adults just ooed and aahd, and marveled at what a good baby she was.

When it was Aunt Nora's turn to come

help Mama, naturally she brought her children. Therefore, with Donald and Orman to play with, we took to the yard, and chased fireflies leaving the baby to the adults. The sounds of the crickets singing in unison, while the bull frogs on the creek bank gave out their croaking clatter, the whippoorwill sang in the trees behind the house, and one lone hoot owl added his voice, to give us a choir. We played in the dark, where all the sounds of nature came together in one chorus, and we were too busy to even notice.

So it was, in 1947 another pink bundle came into our lives. There were now five girls. God had not given our farmer Daddy a son as yet, although his disappointment never showed, one wonders during his quiet times of reflection when he was behind the plow he didn't do some complaining.

He was still working alone accept for some hired hands occasionally for harvest. However God doesn't make mistakes, and he was not any less a man for fathering girls instead of boys.

CHAPTER 6

Having a shortage of beds had not occurred to me. I knew where I would lay down at night, so I did not think too much about where anyone else slept. Eventually Daddy added a room onto the back of the shanty we referred to as a lean-to. He moved the kitchen stove and table to the new addition, and then replaced it with a full bed where the kitchen once had been.

In what we called the living room, a studio couch or a divan which let out to become a bed, yet by any stretch of the imagination it did not sleep like one. Also in the living room was Mama and Daddy's bed. The front door on the south side of the living room led to a porch that extended across the full length of the front of the house. The house was high off the ground so the steps down to the ground were rather steep. As were homes of that era, built on the edge of what would become the road, supported on blocks, one could crawl under the house from one side to the other.

The house was built in the 1800's and would have been warmer had it been built with logs. Instead, it was a clapboard house, meaning boards overlapped with the next, with plaster in the joints. Then each one who owned the house had hung wallpaper to help contain the heat, thus it had several layers of paper on the walls. Birds, rats, chickens, dogs and cats came to live under the house during winter.

On the West side of the living room, was another room equal in size to the small living room. In it were two beds and a trunk that held Mama's treasures from her life in Michigan, as well as seasonal clothes. Across the trunk was a crocheted doily scarf and setting on the scarf was a ceramic statue of a deer restfully lying on its side with its proud head tilted upward. I was told it was unbreakable but that is another story.

Today I remember a story that has taken me through storms, which are a common occurrence where we live. Though I try to have common sense and take cover when the situation calls for us to get into a safe place, I am not afraid. I've often said, "I have no sense of fear" but I truly believe it was an act I saw my father do once that has so instilled in me that "everything is going to be all right" that I believe everything will be all right.

Tennessee was known for its electrical storms as Daddy called them; more lightning, thunder and wind than twister that seem so prevalent today. It was a late afternoon in the spring when such a storm was brewing. We had no such thing as a storm house, and really nowhere to go to wait out the storm. The Shanty was not a safe place from strong winds, but that was all we had.

The wind was whistling in every crack of window and door. Eventually the back door to the Shanty blew open from the fierce winds. As children will, we let out a blood curdling scream when we sensed the fear of what the storm could do.

Daddy calmly but hurriedly ran to the kitchen, shoved the chrome table against the door and instructed us to get on top of the table while he leaned against the door to give it more weight against the howling winds. While we whimpered and cried he kept saying, "It will be over in a few minutes". We listened and again he would say, "Oh it will be gone in a little while". I remember us calming down with each promise he made. I for sure did and my sisters probably did too as we were all young and whatever Daddy said was true, since he knew what he was talking about.

Just as he said, the storm did finally calm down as storms will and moved on out of our area. However it did leave me forever with a calm spirit that everything will be all right. I feel for those who went through tornados when they were younger and saw their parents panic, thus leaving them with a deep rooted fear even today.

The Shanty, then also reminds me of a storm that did pass, and remained a safe home to the growing family of girls for a few more years to come.

CHAPTER 7

"Time to get up girls, Girls, The bus will be here soon. Better get up!" Mama sang as she called to us in the early morning when it was still very dark outside.

In the background, coming from the kitchen was the sound of the radio. "Martha White self-rising flour with hot rise plus" being sung by Bill Monroe and his band. Each morning while we were getting dressed we heard the commercial coming from the radio which was tuned to WSM 650 out of Nashville where the Grand Ole Opry was broadcast on Saturday nights.

I was seven, in second grade that year. I had longed to go to school. When Dean had started school in the fall of 1945 as her birthday fell too late in the year when she turned six. I waited for her to come home each day to ask her if the teachers had said I could go the next day. Each day her answer was no and she and mother tried to explain, "Doris, you aren't old enough yet!" Somehow, I thought I was as old as Dean but I had to settle with their answer. That did not keep me from dreaming, praying and hoping that soon I would be going.

I thought Dean was the smartest person in the world. She didn't say much but her heart was tender and always kind.

My prayer had been answered. I had gone to school a full year and was now in second grade.

With Mama's prodding, and singing out reminders, we reluctantly pulled our bodies up to dash around getting ready for school. We washed our face in a warm pan of water to remove the sleep from our eyes and oils from our face, raked through our hair and reached for the dress we had worn the day before. "It isn't dirty yet," Mother would say. "You can wear it twice, before it needs to be washed."

We accepted what she said, but as we got older, we noticed that our friends did not wear the same dress for two days in a row. It was then we protested. She still had her way; we hung our dress up after each wear, and waited a couple days before wearing it again. Somehow, it made a difference.

There was an unquenchable need in me to be near Daddy. I wonder if this is a general feeling most daughters have. Maybe I longed to be Daddy's special little girl, but outwardly at least it never happened. Each morning in my young years, I inched backwards to stand in front of him so he could tie the belt of my cotton flour sack dress. He sat near the table while Mama cooked breakfast. Therefore, we always knew where to find him. It was great just having him touch my dress; at least he was close for a moment. A hug would have been nice, or an exchange of words but there was neither. Somehow I longed for affirmation that never came.

"No one can tie my belt like you can Daddy!" I would exclaim as I moved away for Dean and Donna who had been in line to have their belts tied as well. There was never a response I was listening for.

Being in second grade did not mean much more than being in first as far as I was concerned. I still enjoyed the school experience. I was not particularly fond of riding the bus however. The fumes from the old noisy gas burning bus, made me ill and often a migraine headache resulted. If I had the headache when I got up in the morning and the pain was excruciating I knew to stay home to get better. Still other times I wanted to go to school so badly I went anyway, only to have the bus driver stop long enough to let me off the bus and vomit. Sometimes it would relieve the pain, other times the school got hold of Daddy to come get me.

"Let me see your pencil", the high school girl asked as I sat by her on the bus ride to school. It was her way of making conversation, but she made me uncomfortable. Daddy had sharpened my pencil the night before with his knife and I had a death grip on it holding it where no one could see the ugly sharpening job. It was rough and ugly as far as I was concerned. One could tell it had not been near an actual pencil sharpener like we had at school, and I did not want her to see any part of my pencil.

She was one from the Robins family who

lived on a farm with her parents, brother, and sister several miles up the road. Being much older, they moved away before I started waking up from my embarrassment and bashfulness. The girls were much older than me, as being in high school when I was only in the second grade making it impossible for me to remember their names..

I said nothing but held my pencil inside the fold of my cotton dress showing her I did not want to reveal to anyone my hideous pencil. She would have understood, and probably had her pencils sharpened by her dad somewhere along the way. However, it was an introduction to my shyness; A shyness that engulfed me when I was in a situation I knew not how to deal with.

It was not only in the 1940's; it was a malady which was mine and difficult to overcome for years into my future. Inferiority! I realized later where it came from, but at seven years of age, who could know the sickening feeling of fear and inferiority had a name. At home around family, I could be myself – the talkative one who sang and had imaginary friends. I was comfortable, my inferiority never showed up until "strangers", and well-meaning people spoke to me.

My teacher was Miss Ladd. She had been my first grade teacher as well as second grade and I was glad to have her with her gentle spirit again. It seemed I lost my shyness when I got to school. Somehow, I felt comfortable there; comfortable enough that the real me came to the surface. I was a fast learner as my comprehension and reading were above average for a second grader. I had a thirst to learn. My reading skills were superb and math not far behind. Therefore, it is reasonable to understand why I had difficulty concentrating on a quiet project such as reading, or coloring at my desk during study period.

"Doris", Miss Ladd spoke in her usually sweet quiet voice as she leaned down close to my ear. Miss Ladd was a stately older woman who was very much at home in a classroom of young children.

"We don't sing during study time", she finished. I did not realize how loud I was, for I thought my song was inside my head not resounding through my clenched jaws and closed mouth.

"OK Ma'am" I said quietly and went back to reading or coloring.

Oh there it was again. That song; It keeps going off in my head. I'm going to think of something else, I promised myself.

"Doris", Miss Ladd leaned down to get my attention. "Sshhh!" she noised with her forefinger against her pursed lips.

I nodded in approval.

Oh God, please help me not to sing out loud. I know, I'll just look out the window and maybe it will go out of my head, I ...

"Doris", Miss Ladd was at my elbow, helping me up this time. "Let's go to the cloak room". (I never did get it figured out why they would call it a cloakroom when all it held was our coats. I never called my coat a cloak)

"Now get your coat and go stand outside on the porch and sing. I want you to sing until you are through then you can come back inside with the rest of us".

She was so kind, how could I get mad at her. So - I did just that. I stood on the porch that cold October day and sang. No, I do not remember the song. Wish I did.

I never told Mama I had been disciplined, I probably should have. Maybe it would have given her an idea about various kinds of punishments. She knew one kind and that was spanking. Not with her hand necessarily, but with anything she could get her hand on. Daddy never raised his hand in discipline, but the look he gave sent us scurrying for cover. It wasn't his whippings we dreaded but the tongue-lashings and words that came from his mouth were always harsh. He did not know how to speak any other way. The bruises that came from being whipped with a stick of wood or a tree switch would eventually heal, but the bruises that came from harsh words would linger on in the heart and memory of each child to adulthood and beyond.

Mama caught them when he was angry,

and we caught them when he was angry and neither of us could always say what we had done to deserve the tongue-lashing.

His voice was gruff. His voice was not gentle. To my listening ears, his answers to my questions made me think I was a nuisance and should not bother him. Once out of innocence, I called him "father". His harshness left a mark that seemed unforgettable and stayed with me for years.

"Don't ever call me that again! Father......There is only one and that is God!"

I had recently heard the word and used it to address him. I probably never would again, but then I was trying the word out. I distinctly remember the scene. We were setting in the car, waiting for Mama who had gone inside Mrs. Lena Reynolds house for a minute. As we waited on her, Linda, Martha and I were in the back seat and then I tried addressing him as father. Needless to say, his words lingered and I had a difficult time with addressing God as father for a long time. As parents we do not know the lasting impact we can have on our children when we are thoughtless with our answering their questions, albeit even innocent ones.

CHAPTER 8

It didn't take long for the cold winds of winter to start coming in every crack of window, wall, door and floor. Heating the wood stove until it was red on one side did little to get the heat in all the rooms.

The door to our west side bedroom of the Shanty had been closed all day to contain the heat in the two rooms where we spent our days. The heat from the kitchen and living room did not travel very far to any room outside where the stoves set. However, the thought was to hopefully open the door about an hour before going to bed so as to ease the bone chilling cold of the below zero temperatures

It was one such winter in 1951 when Grandmamma Chapman died. (Addie Hodge Chapman) She had breast cancer and had struggled for a while. I remember visiting her during the summer or fall when she was being taken care of by her children and Granddaddy. I remember her gentleness. Seeing her so seldom, I have very few memories. Sitting on her lap when she visited us in the summer, she would comb and braid my hair.

There are occasions in everyone's life when a whiff of a slight smell, or a song, or a touch - something that comes to remind us of another place and another time. That's what happens when someone combs or touches my hair, I think of her and it is wonderful. I remember how peaceful and gentle she was as she talked with Mama and held me while combing my hair. I was close to her for a few minutes anyway.

It is amazing how our elderly grandparents never really carried on a conversation with us. It must not have been something they did. Maybe I asked too many questions for them to answer. I've often wondered. I hungered for conversation and interaction with adults I was familiar with anyway.

On occasion I would "slip off" down the hill to Grandma Tanner's house. I'd just go for a visit, but would soon return to the house as there was no meaningful conversation to be found. Oh yes, we may have talked a little, but nothing I could relate to. Other than Grandpa showing me his sundial clock on the porch and even at that I never did understand even though I thought it was intriguing. I wanted to spend the night and get to sleep on that high feather bed. I thought she could make up the prettiest beds I had ever seen. In the two room house my Dad had built for them, the kitchen was one and the other was their living room combination bed room. As each of them slept in a different bed, I guess to have grandchildren spend the night was out of the question.

Anyway, it was too cold to get the whole family to the funeral as Daddy and Mama had to find a ride with someone to even get through the snow and weather to Paris, Tennessee where she was to be buried. I don't remember how our days went with Grandma and Grandpa Tanner being in charge. I do remember how lonely it was especially at night because Mama wasn't there. I would soon be eleven and had never been without her. None of us had. It didn't take us long to go to sleep when we did lay down, leaving the wood stove and heating the house to Grandma and Grandpa Tanner.

Winters repeated themselves with very little variation from one winter to another. On what seemed to be the coldest day of the winter, neighbors gathered to kill hogs. I guess I understand now the meat would not spoil as quickly as it would have on warmer days.

I was always excited about the meat we would get to eat, Fresh meat; something besides chicken. A few mornings after the hog kill day, the meat had been salted down for preservation, or hung in the smoke house to cure, we would have tenderloin and homemade biscuits and gravy. Oh my, my mouth waters just thinking about the bounty after hog killing time. It happened in most winters, and meat was plentiful for most of the year.

Mostly we tried to stay warm. The snow winds blew and the countryside became a beautiful blanket of white, with tall evergreens standing high and gently blowing in the winter wind. Each field on the open land seemed a continuous layer of white, interrupted only by the dead bushes at the outer skirts of the field along the fence row.

The cattle stayed around the barn, eating from their stalls where Daddy had placed hay. They drank from containers in the barnyard where Daddy had poured hot water to melt the ice.

And inside the house were five little girls, with two parents who were doing their best to keep a roof over our head and food on the table, with sufficient clothes to keep us warm on those cold winter days. The five little girls had no idea there may be different circumstances in other homes, nearby or anywhere in the world. We were shielded from the dangers that may have lurked outside our door or the red light ladies a few miles away, or the men who made illegal liquor or corn whisky a few miles up the road.

We were busy doing what little girls do. Play without a care in the world, not knowing there was a world outside the little shanty house where we lived. Only God could paint a picture like that of innocents. A big contrast really, of parents keeping their struggles to themselves while their children giggled with delight at whatever they found to do enjoying each other's company on cold winter days.

"Girls it's getting late and tomorrow is a school day", Mama would say. It wasn't late for me. I seemed to be a night owl, not being able to go to sleep when we were told to. Morning always came too early.

"Do I have to?" I whined knowing the bed would still be ice cold. "I'm not going first tonight", I added boldly.

"I went first last night," Donna chimed in.

"No you didn't, I did" was Dean's cry.

Dean and I could never seem to win an argument. Donna pulled rank on us but even at that, Mama usually intervened and the three of us went to bed at the same time.

We thought nothing of sleeping three and even four to a bed, our small frames seem to fit very well together. As far as we were concerned, that was the picture in households through out the world. Martha and Linda wanted to sleep next to Dean. I didn't care. Sleeping several in a bed afforded us a time of togetherness. A time when we shared secrets, we forgot by the next morning we had promised not to tell. It was a time of unwinding after our day. It was a time of giggling at nothing and everything. It was a wonderful time of just being next to each other; a time that is still embedded in the heart of each of us.

Even though we closed our eyes to sleep, it was a different story on the other side of the wall where Mama and Daddy were.

"There is plenty room on the strip of land up behind the house here, that would be a pretty place to build a new house". Mama offered at any opportunity she had. He heard but never gave her anything to build hopes on. He knew something had to give and was working on a plan but did not acknowledge she was right.

CHAPTER 9

Daddy was the fourth of six children. I really cannot imagine the era in which he was born and the conditions of the times, or the general lack of display of affection to each other. History gives us a glimpse, but here was a man who had lived it. Survival was the concern of people in the early 1900's.

He was much like his father, in that he was a quiet man. If a conversation developed between Grandpa and another person, most likely he did not initiate it. Daddy was the same. I took it for granted it was normal that men did not communicate with their children. Without realizing it, he had an unspoken way that told us not to go take his hand, or sit in his lap. I hung on his every word as he talked about the land and his progress of the day. He cleared new ground. It was a tedious job he accomplished by himself.

"I fought a rattle snake all over that hillside today", he would say. Immediately my imagination went to work. I could see him fighting all right, only I saw it this way - the snake was standing up and together they were duke-in' it out on the hillside!

What he was saying was the snake had refused to die. Regardless of what instrument he used to kill the snake, it would not give up without a fight.

In the next few days, Daddy talked of a

copper head snake that got mad because he had disturbed its nest, and again "I had to fight that copper head all over that hillside!" He finally did get the new ground field cleared, and it became a grazing ground for the cows.

While he was working the hillside, his cry for help had Mama running to his aide. He used the mules to help him pull tree stumps out of the ground. For some reason one of the mules kicked him in the side and broke a rib or ribs. She had to help him get to the house where he was unable to do anything for a while. Mama brought the team home and they had a few days of rest until he was able to go back to the field.

I'm sure he was like other fathers, but I had no frame of reference. His quietness and reluctance to carry on a conversation with anyone was a handicap in some ways or that is the way I perceived him anyway. Now to talk to a male visitor, church men, the pastor or his brothers, he had no problem carrying on a conversation, so maybe he wasn't as shy as I have accepted.

He didn't want to vote, but he could tell you who was running and all about them. He was a Democrat, but I'm not sure if he knew what side the local politicians were on. However he may have because all we heard was the last name of the Politian and in front of the name (if he didn't like him) was "Old"…..

However to talk with his daughters it was difficult even though we craved his attention. I knew he had a temper. Get out of the way George when he was mad!

In the beginning I had no thought of making him face himself, however that is how it ended. The story goes like this: Once during the winter when he was doing something around the house that required pliers, he could not get them to work properly. There was no Wal-Mart to run to, so he used the same ole ones and did not think about it until he needed it again.

If truth was known, he did not have new or proper tools to do many things which needed repair. Trying to get them to work for him and nothing he did helped; He got furious with the pliers. With a few choice words that were not profanity, he went to the front door, and with his arm in a baseball pitcher's stance, he threw the pliers as hard as he could down into the yard where it landed in five-inch deep snow. We could say they rested under the big shade tree where we spent many summer days resting from the heat, until the spring.

It took a few weeks for the spring sun to melt the great snow that had fallen several times during the winter. I cannot forget the anger I saw coming from Daddy that day he threw the faulty pliers away but somehow it did not affect me. I just knew I would do anything to keep him from venting that anger on me.

I had gone to the spring for water. I did a lot of musing while doing the task of bringing water up the steep hill. Thinking comes easy when walking with a bucket of water, so the pliers in the yard came to mind.

I walked away from the normal path, picked up the pliers, and went into the house with the water. I set the water on the water shelf and proceeded to find Daddy. He happened to be close to the house so I waited for him to come inside I walked up to him, in front of everyone, and said, "Daddy, look what I found down in the yard. Are these yours?"

The look on his face is still vivid in my mind today. He smiled that famous grin which often turned into a laugh. Only this time he took the pliers, grinned and walked away. The look let me know he had instant recall of the day he threw them away and the disposition with which he did it.

I do not know why, but I never seemed to notice his character traits. What I read of his attention to Mama was not always the way it was. I did not have much to compare. Mama could have used a friend to talk with about his jealousy and his meanness. Maybe she did talk to Aunt Nora. They were the best of friends and I believe she became a confidant to Mama as she poured out her frustrations. As it was, they had married brothers and if anyone would understand she would!

CHAPTER 10

"Girls, hurry up and get dressed. Today is wash day," Mama called in a singsong voice we were so accustomed to.

It was summer and washday meant we would go to Grandma Tanner's who lived down by the creek and beside the spring and probably stay all day. Daddy had built the house for his parents when they were no longer able to work the fields. It was a two-room log house, with two beds in the living quarters with a fireplace.

Their house set in the valley under a grove of trees that grew up the hillside. A graveled drive way connected the land to the road. The spring, where we got water, was under the same hill around the bend. The big bluff made an overhang where the spring with its cool crystal clear water flowed from under the rocky bluff. The spring branch ran on one side of their house and flowed into the rock creek, on the west side of their property. I wish I could paint the picture that is still vivid in my mind.

Three big barrels set under the roof ledge on the back porch of our house. When it failed to rain, and the barrels were empty, the next thing was to go to the creek where water was plentiful and do the wash using Grandma's big wash kettle.

However when it did rain, she did the wash at home where it was more convenient. It was usually a one man job, but we did help hang the clothes on the line and pray the sun kept shining so we could get some fresh smelling clothes off the line later in the day.

But going to the Creek, Mama loaded the little wagon with a week's worth of wash for seven people and down the road we went, helping Mama keep the clothes in the wagon.

We each helped her get water into the kettle. I thought we would never get it filled. She sorted the clothes on the ground while shooing away the cats and chickens at the same time. Grandma had cats, that had cats, and each cat told the neighborhood cats she would take in strangers, so to count the ones who came to stay would not be possible.

"But there's probably a hundred," I suggested. They did not turn me off, but Mother on the other hand was. In fact, she hated cats. She did not want one near her, near her house, or in her house for sure.

Once in the summer of 1949, I thought Mama had forgotten my birthday. Washday could have been the reason she kept quiet but I was excited to be turning nine years old that day, June 9. I never had a party, so that didn't bother me. It was my golden birthday no less. Donna and Dean remembered when I told them it was my birthday. I just wanted someone to remember that I was born that day nine years ago! Linda was quick in her almost five-year-old way to encourage me that my birthday was important.

The wash took most of the day. Mother stirred the clothes in the boiling water inside the big kettle, took them from the water to scrub the clothes by hand on the scrub board that leaned against the insides of another tub, rinsed them in a second tub of water, and then took them to the line to dry. I kept listening for a sign that she remembered having me nine years ago. Nothing.

I had no idea Mama had made a pan of golden brown cornbread on Grandma's stove and it was waiting for her.

"Girls" she called. "Donna, Dean, Doris, Linda and Martha" she sang the words again. Martha was only two years old, but wherever her sisters were she was.

We stopped what we were doing to go to the wash kettle. In her hand were the cornbread and six glasses. We followed her to the spring in the shade of the big bluff where we set down and prepared ourselves for lunch. The springhouse kept the milk cold. Oh yes, cold! Mama reached into the springhouse and pulled out a big jug of buttermilk.

We set down on the ground and she served us each a glass of buttermilk. The spoons she had brought from Grandma's were dispersed among us, and then she sliced the bread. Buttermilk and cornbread was our lunch. My birthday was mentioned in passing, but otherwise no fanfare.

"I'll bet you are the only one in the world that had a picnic of milk and bread on her birthday!" Mama said with enthusiasm and a laugh. We laughed with her, for it was true - no one I knew ever had and probably never would. I liked it when they sang Happy Birthday to me. I did not know I was underprivileged. To me it was a time when the lens of my memory snapped a picture I still have tucked away in my thoughts today and recall often.

Later on another such wash day, we had been going to church since I was about twelve. I was fascinated with the singings, preaching and baptizing. So fascinated that I'd gather Linda and Martha and have we would have church. Of course I was always the preacher; I don't know why, unless it was because I was in charge. I didn't give them a chance to; I was forever the instigator and leader.

We were finished helping mama fill the wash pot, and she had not asked anything of us in a while, so I decided to have a baptizing in the spring branch. I had heard the words; I had watched as the preacher put people under, I knew just how to do it. So, I enlisted Linda and Martha to help me. Linda was about 9, and Martha was almost 6 or a little over. (I stand to be corrected on any of our ages by the way.) So together they trotted off to retrieve a cat. My instructions were for each of them to bring a cat that needed to be baptized.

Momentarily they returned; each one with a cat in their arms. Per my instructions I had them stand on the bank of the spring branch and wait 'til I ask for the animal. I proceeded to get in the water that was a little more than ankle deep, and had Martha hand me her cat.

"In the name of the Father, the Son and the Holy Ghost, I baptize this……." I don't remember what I called him, but I took the squirming cat and pushed him under. I didn't intend to hold him under so long. I turned him loose as I brought my hands out of the water. To my dismay, and horror the cat stayed in the water and floated on down the branch toward the creek.

I tried to explain to my little sisters not to tell anyone. I did not want to admit my good intentions had gone wrong, but they were witnesses to my plan gone sour, so I had to make a pact they wouldn't tell.

Linda quickly dropped her cat to the ground and looked toward me in wide eyed dismay.

Hindsight is 20/20. Now I know Mama would not have cared, and Grandma would never miss it. She had so many they didn't even have a name. Looking back I realize I was probably the first one who told on myself.

CHAPTER 11

It was June and the summer chores were still ahead of us. We were getting old enough to help pull weeds from the garden and corn patch in the field beside the house. Without giving it much thought Donna and Dean had already been working around the house giving Mama some needed relief in the kitchen for sure.

We played outside as much as possible. Mama assured us that the sun would make us pretty. So, even at an early age, the female in us wanted just that. We had heard a little about Hollywood and Betty Grable, or Greer Garson. We also knew stories like Cinderella, or Repunzel. Taking her at her word, we did play outside until our chores called us to attention.

We begged to go to the creek and play as much as we could to get relief from the hot weather. None of us could swim at that time, but we loved pretending anyway. The spring rains always left a good swimming hole and often we'd walk barefoot on the rough rocks up the creek bed or down the creek bed to see if there might be another hole the rains had washed out. The creek ran the length of the farm so we never had to venture far from home to go swimming and play in the creek until Mama called us home.

Daddy always warned us to be careful of the creek critters such as snakes and terrapins for sure. "If a terrapins gets hold of your toes," he warned, "he won't turn loose until it thunders again!" We looked at him like "you got to be kidding". He looked serious enough so we believed him. Needless to say, we were sure we did not get near one, for our minds could visualize it never thundering again and we'd have to live with a turtle on our foot. Oh the tales we heard and took to heart.

"Don't get in the deep water until you learn how to swim!" was another one. The truth is no one showed us how to swim, and now we realize to learn to swim one must be in more than knee deep water! Oh the stories we share of those early days.

The day came when Daddy started thinking more seriously about the need for a larger house. Maybe that wasn't his first inkling; however he was more vocal now than before. Since adding the lean-to on the west side of the shanty still did not given enough space with five growing girls, the need to do something different had been weighing on his mind.

Though she had learned to tread softly with Daddy, Mama urged him on many occasions to make plans to build a bigger house on the land. He was preoccupied with the business of farming and doing it alone except for some help he could pick up during harvest. As long as he had a place to lay down his weary body at the end of the day, he did not see the same needs his wife did. She ran a tight ship and did it well so he did not notice that their daughters were sleeping sometime four to a bed.

"There is plenty room on this strip of land up behind the house. It would be a pretty place for a new house." She offered at any opportunity she had. He heard but never offered any hope.

It was late so she closed her eyes and drifted off to sleep.

Money does not flow into farmers hands during winter. With Hay cut in late fall, and put in the barn loft, there was a period of waiting for winter to pass. As the land was resting from the summer crops, Daddy decided to go north to Joliet, Illinois where Mama's sister Louise and her husband lived. Uncle Charlie was in construction work and could always use a good hand. It was during the evenings they made a blueprint for the house that was to replace the shanty.

Farming isn't easy, but Mama seemed resilient somehow and finished the chores with determination while he was away. We helped by gathering eggs and watching the younger children. Once more, I wonder if Mama's dreams continued of a better life or had she given up hope. I know she read magazines and true romance stories, and had a good picture of what another life might look like, distorted as the magazines may have portrayed it. Whether the life she dreamed would have been a better romantic life, I am not sure. Mama was living life however, one that many women of her era lived. She was not alone. Having others around her who were farmer's wives, did not keep her from dreaming of a life unlike what she had.

There were no telephones in those days, and Electricity for Long Branch was still a few years away. Mama waited for a letter from Daddy to give her news about how things were going in Illinois and when he had planned to come home.

Winter brought darkness much too soon, and the oil lamps and lanterns were lighted to dispel the darkness from room to room as needed. Getting homework was no problem as we had learned to focus our eyes on the light filtered page of our tablet.

The house was always cold, as one heating stove was to heat up the entire house. With the chores done, Mama occupied her girls. When Daddy was not making demands, Mama was able to play, and play we did.

Especially during the day, when snow gave us a day home from school, we played. It was good not to have to brave the cold winter weather in Tenn. In fact we did not mind for it was good to stay home with Mama.

So from a game around the table, to cutting out people in magazines and making paper dolls, Mama was ingenious in her skills to keep us occupied. I always thought Mama was the smartest person I ever saw.

Daddy came home for Christmas, but was soon gone back to Illinois to work a while longer. By February 1950, he returned to start the planting season. He found fertile soil on a hill in full view of the sun. There he planted seedlings of which he would later transplant into Mama's garden. He covered the seedlings with dirt, then the whole bed with canvas cloth to protect the seedlings as they grew, and then waited as the sun and rain did the rest.

He was excited about clearing the land for the new house. In each spare minute, he cut down trees and cleared underbrush where the house would set. He took the team of mules to pull up stubborn stumps and roots. Then he took the plow and started making furrows where the foundation and basement would be. It was not easy for one man to do, but he hung in there and worked hard using what tools he had. He used dynamite to break up the rock and roots that hindered his digging. Occasionally his brother Clyde came to assist him along with Grandpa their father. He being old was not much help I'm sure. Hopefully he was beneficial in getting tools and equipment for them which was out of reach.

The booming sounds of the dynamite exploding kept going on for weeks at a time. I just remember thinking *I will be glad when that noise is over.* The fumes from the blasting dynamite left a putrid smell in the air that made me nauseous. It probably had the similar effects on everyone including Daddy, but it was not discussed. I had migraine headaches anyway, so the smell of the dynamite blasts brought on days of headaches.

We were like children anticipating Christmas as we watched the house go up.

Electricity was in the community by the early 1950's. Daddy had brought an electrical cable into the kitchen of the Shanty to give us electricity for the radio. Once during his lunch break from farming or building, he was setting in the kitchen of the shanty listening to the Lone Ranger. An electric radio was a novelty.

I guess this was the first time I saw Mama in her girlish prankster character. Sometime she would engage us in her pranks but this one was hers all the way. She admonished us to be quiet.

"Sshhh!" she would say with pursed lips as she edged closer to the open window where Daddy sat with his back toward the window. On the radio program, the cavalry had set out to catch the bad guy, when in the middle of the intense climax as the guns were blaring, the sound of the horses hoofs against the gravel, the music getting louder, and Daddy's blood was rushing in anticipation of the next move and who would do the shooting, Mama stood at one end of the broom, and pushed the handle end through the window and into Daddy's ribs just at the most intense moment. He let out a yelp as he jumped up and looked around. We rolled in the grass roaring with laughter as the scene played out before us. Daddy did not do much laughing at the time, but his children enjoyed the memory it was to make. When I think of Mama, I smile at her love for play.

CHAPTER 12

Daddy had been staying in a room behind the stage at the church in Illinois when he went there to work for Uncle Charlie. They were in a revival but he didn't bother to attend. Naturally we were and are known for our loudness in church service, so he was hearing everything even if he wasn't in the actual church.

His heart became convicted. So one night without anyone around him, he began crying and repented of his sins and negligence for putting God on the back burner of his life and being too busy to take his children to church.

When he came home after his few months in Illinois, I will always remember the difference in him. I was still young, but I do remember we started thanking the Lord for our meal and His blessings before we ate. If Mama didn't pray, he did. I loved hearing him pray.

When Grandpa Chapman visited, I loved hearing him pray before meals as well. There was something about his prayers that have lingered and often when I pray before a meal I find myself repeating a line he used, "Help us to be grateful for this and all thy blessings."

Not having a car, we went to church as often as we could. Donna, Dean and I were old enough to walk. Mama saw that we were dressed well and had Sunday shoes that pinched our feet like crazy. I've decided it was what they were made of then, or another thought - they could have been handed down from an older sister who had outgrown them, or from a neighbor. Either way they looked better than our work shoes. So we made a decision to start walking in our work/everyday shoes and when we got in sight of the church we would put our shoes in the weeds beside the road out of sight. They were in a bag of course. Then on our way home we retrieved our shoes and walked home.

People offered to take us home, but we had to refuse for we sure couldn't tell them our shoes were beside the road. I'm sure that didn't happen many times, but it is a memory that stays with us.

For revivals or special occasions, our precious distant cousin and Brother in the Lord, Lawrence Self came by for us to ride - hay-ride style on the back of his big truck. I was terrified of getting up on that big truck. It looked so high off the ground for my little frame. I don't remember but surely someone helped me on. And then we'd go back home on the hay-ride. It wasn't just the sisters and me, but many others around the community who could not have gone otherwise.

He was so big hearted; he offered to bring us home many times when we had to retrieve our shoes. As great as it might have been not to walk, we had to say no.

Eventually Daddy got a car and we loaded the seven of us in and went to Sunday school and church on Sunday night. The Pastor I remember best, for he was there during my growing years, was E. L. Carpenter. I paid attention to his preaching and remember one sermon especially where he used the scripture from Revelations 3:20 *"Behold, I stand at the door, and knock: if any man hear my voice, and open the door, I will come in to him, and will sup with him, and he with me."* I could even remember the scripture reference.

During the summer of 1952 soon after my twelfth birthday Bro. Carpenter had invited two young women to hold a revival. It was well attended, as their preaching was evangelistic. Outside men and boys covered the hillside and listened. I believe they wanted Jesus, but it was not cool for the men to be Christians. There were few men inside the church, but men like Daddy was not deterred by those who chose to stay on the outside.

Each night the altar was filled with people who wanted to be saved from their sins. Each night there was no pleading for anyone to come to the altar, the spirit of the Lord would draw people to acknowledge their need for Him.

I knew I couldn't last much longer. I sat with the pastor's daughter Sue each night. This particular night I urged her to go with me to pray. She refused but I knew I had to go. During my prayer I was reminded of something I had stolen from Donna. This was the years when we saved box tops, or tablet covers and sent them off for things we may not have gotten otherwise.

Donna had got a ring with her savings and one day I decided to try it on and it was my intentions to return it. Oh me, somewhere I misplaced it, but lied each time she ask everyone about it. "I haven't seen it I promise!" I lied feeling lower than low each time I spoke up.

I felt like the Lord would not hear me accept I confessed my sins. Being so young there was only one sin I had to confess. In my innocence and childlikeness, I went to Mama. I fell into her arms crying so hard she could hardly understand me. I told her what I had done and she said, "I think you need to go to Donna and tell her."

For some reason I don't remember going to Donna that night, maybe she was in the altar as well. I went back to finish my prayer and as the scripture declares, I was a new creature in Christ. "Old things were passed away and all things had become new." I had no past to speak of - only a bright future filled with hope. I did not understand everything which had happened to me then, and it would take years until I recognized a Love I had never felt before.

It was in 1978 while at a retreat in Wagoner Oklahoma, I was bathed in the love of the Father I had been looking for all my life. My self-esteem had always been at the bottom. I had no confidence in myself or what I might be able to accomplish. As far as I was concerned, I couldn't be a good Mother, Wife, or friend. I was no good. I didn't know enough to help anyone. God helped me to come to terms with the phrases that rolled around in my head occasionally, often being repeated; "Dummy", or "lame brain" It was a word I had become familiar with and its connotation had a big negative on my self-esteem and self-worth. It was spoken in anger I know, but as children when it is spoken by a parent it sticks to the brain as though it has been doused with super glue. A parent knows what they're talking about right? I must be dumb or stupid - or they would not have said such.

And it takes God to remove the word and its meaning from the brain and heart. I did do some pretty stupid things - for I was a free spirit and tried out new things regardless of the warnings from Mama or the consequences.

Psalms 139 came alive to me. I devoured it. Other Scriptures also came alive and I grasped them and took them into my spirit and brain to replace the ugly word I had held on to for so long.

From there I looked into the mirror and was able to see the real woman I was; the one that God saw when He looked at me. I came to terms with the idea, 'God don't make junk' and without being able to put it into words, that's exactly how I had felt for a long time. Oh yes I was an evangelist - and God blessed my efforts. However there may have been greater results had I saw myself as God saw me; Able to do all things through Christ who strengthens me.

I began seeing in me what God had created and knew what I could become in Him. After I accepted His unconditional love He challenged me to teach His word. I lived in the Bible for several months, absorbing and eating everything I read. He doesn't make junk I finally digested. He makes beauty? I was not a Cinderella, but I was not ugly either. Seeing myself as He saw me, the apple of His eye, was liberating.

I had started evangelizing in 1960, much unprepared. The Lord blessed in several revivals in Alabama, and then when the call came from Brother J.C. Wood in Tupelo Miss., we moved west from Alabama. Still not prepared in scripture knowledge, I obeyed and scared though I was the revival lasted several weeks, and the house was filled each night. We sang I gave the Word and in my willingness God sent the increase.

However it was 1979 in Waggoner, Oklahoma and I had been reborn in a sense. I had found the Father. The best way I can explain it is I knew Jesus. I had invited Him into my heart in 1952. Unlearned as I was I'm sure I failed many times and displeased Him. However He also saw this day in August 1979, when I would actually look up from my bewilderment, depression and hole I had dug for myself to hide in, and see my Maker, God Almighty, my Creator, Prince of Peace, and Everlasting Father.

I had such a hunger to give back to Him who had been so willing to give me peace and assurance and acceptance. I knew again I was not ready to give the Word, I still knew so very little; so each for several months when I got the kids out the door for school, I started reading the Bible. I fasted 1 week and again 3 weeks, eating the Word for my sustenance

From that day doors began opening that would not have opened had I not had a new relationship with Him.

From North Carolina to California and many places in-between; from Canada to Europe, from the Bahama Islands, Jamaica, Barbados and Porto Rico, then into Central America. I think of what I might have missed had I not prayed that night long ago in 1952 as well as my visitation in 1978..

That overwhelming love of my Father caused me to see my own father whom I had desired to know, as a man who needed love himself. As I learned about his upbringing, I realized love was not displayed in his home, and he did not know how to show anyone else love. My Father, helped me forgive my earthly father and it felt good.

CHAPTER 13

It took Daddy awhile to build the house even with Uncle Charlie coming to help with the rafters and roof, but all the inside work and some of the outside was left up to Daddy. I'm sure Mama helped while we were away at school. It was an education for all of us learning new words like, sheetrock, rafters, or masking tape.

During the building process before installing the sheetrock, an electrician had come to wire the house so that each room would have its own light. My goodness, it was more than my 11 year old mind could comprehend, even though Daddy had run an extension cord into the kitchen of the Shanty so that room would have light.

After the outside walls were up, and the rooms were portioned, the unfinished rooms became a playground of sorts for Donna, Dean and me. We loved standing at the Radio, listening to the Grand Ole Opry and singing every song we heard. We did a good job pretending we were there on stage with the likes of Kitty Wells or Roy Acuff or even Bill Monroe. We just knew had we had the right exposure we could have been famous singers on the Grand Ole Opry stage.

We had learned to harmonize while harvesting the peanuts the fall before. Along with Daddy, we pulled the peanuts from the root of the vine and started singing. It seemed the most natural thing to do – to sing while we worked. As a rule, Daddy's lips were puckered for whistling, so we started singing with him. Dean took the lead, I sang the high tenor art, and Donna came in with the most beautiful alto and Daddy chimed in with the bass. To say he was pleased is an understatement. He was excited. He heard his children harmonize their voices and he was delighted. It was one of those times he was able to show his pride in his children. From there we sang every chance we could get.

Moving into the new house was a process we took several days to do as the farm chores had to continue in spite of our excitement to get moved in.

There were six rooms in the new house, with a separate kitchen and dining room. Mama and Daddy had their privacy at last. Donna and I shared a room and Dean, Linda and Martha shared the other one. There was an unfinished upstairs where two extra bedrooms were planned. The unfinished basement served as a good place to play on rainy days as well as a cellar to keep all the jars of vegetables and jellies Mother managed to preserve during the summer. And even though we had electricity there was no running water or indoor plumbing. That was not to be until many years later.

Eventually, the shanty was torn down and clearing the ground was one of the next priorities. I was too young to realize we had made memories while living in the shanty that would serve us a lifetime. Not having the visual of the shanty made our memories even more precious as we held them close and shared them with each other often.

"Do you remember the switch tree that was behind the old house?" one will ask, and the rest of us chime in with "Oh yes, and do you remember Mama having us get our own switch when she was going to punish us?"

That was not totally the way we recall it, but it was close enough to bring us laughter again and again. We lived; we loved, and dreamed dreams of another time someday, far away, as we played around the shanty, but times were about to change now that it was a memory.

CHAPTER 14

Mama made the best of her life. She was often depressed. Menopause was especially difficult on women in the 1950's with little medical knowledge as to the changes taking place in a woman's body or what she needed for that matter. I feel sure, in retrospect, she didn't feel well a great deal of times, but for sure there was no time to give in to her feelings and lay down. In her heart, she may have loved to hide away, but outwardly she moved on.

As children, we were not aware of the dreams she still held on to, we would not have understood anyway. I wonder if she looked back at her home in Michigan. I'm sure she remembered Mrs. Crumbaker. They wrote letters and kept in touch. I watched as Mama tore into an envelope that held the letters from Mrs. Crumbaker. She read. She remembered. She dreamed of the city, the park a few blocks away, the market down the street, and the friendships she had gained.

In her preparing the move to Tennessee, she got rid of all her electrical appliance not thinking she would need them in the hill country of Tennessee. I wonder if she was aware of the hard times she would face. Did she ever think of Whippoorwill hollow? Was she aware that the Shanty was small and drafty? I wonder also if she took Daddy's word and from his enthusiasm of the future, she never looked back, or was she hoping things between them would change once they moved out of the big city to a more simple way of life.

She did bring some of her treasures she had bought for the house. The thing I remember most was a ceramic deer that was in a resting position on a trunk that had made its way from Michigan to the Shanty. I heard her tell someone that it was unbreakable as they admired it. She was so proud of that deer. He was beautifully painted with a touch of gray but mostly brown with some white spots, his eyes so realistic and his ears perked up as if he was on alert for danger.

One of day when we lived in the Shanty and I was trying to conquer my little world, I went into the bedroom that stayed closed off during the day in winter, to look at the deer. The room was crowded, with two full beds and almost every square inch on the floor was taken up with stuff she had no room for anywhere else. I looked at the deer and thought, "She said it was unbreakable, I wonder if it really is!" Mama had warned me several times, for some reason, to keep my hands off the deer.

For the life of me, my little pea brain did not grasp the warning. I bent over and slowly put my hands under the deer. It was heavy! Then I slid my arms further under him so as to get a good trip on him. Standing in an upright position, I decided to see if it was unbreakable. Oh my, when it hit the floor, it broke in several places. My feelings were mixed. I had disobeyed, now I was in trouble, I didn't want to tell her and in my immaturity I decided not to tell anyone. Duh! A broken deer on the floor that was formerly setting on a flat surface could not get to the floor by himself.

Today I'd say *if only life had a remote control. I'd go back a few minutes and run from the room and let my temptation to hold the deer pass.*

My punishment was one of those times, the switch tree was used. Mama had given the tree its name by the mere fact she pulled one (or had us to) to switch the legs and backside of the sinner.

"Go to the switch tree and get a limb so I can wear you out!" she would bark orders when she was mad. If we were reluctant, she would send one of the other sisters, but she did get her switch. Today someone could report her to SCAN, or the authorities, but then we thought nothing of getting our legs switched. It did hurt but she made her point. "If you tell a lie, you get punished. If you disobey you will be punished."

I figured she could have given me away many times, had she known who would take me!!!

On occasion Saturdays was for shopping in town day. Daddy hitched the team to the wagon, other neighbors had done the same and farmers from miles converged on the city of Erin to buy their staple items. It took most of a whole day. Always remembering to bring us back a treat, we waited for the sound of the wagon wheels crunching gravel as it neared our house, and we jumped with glee as we waited for our candy bar or vanilla wafer.

    Putting myself in her place, I think she looked for the best and prettiest sacks the flour came in. In doing so, she would take the flour sack material and make someone a dress. Even though she may have wanted the material for herself, the needs of her little girls came first. Often it took several trips to town to get enough of the flour sack material to make what she wanted. Come school time in August we each had a new dress to wear the first day. It was not new after that first day, but we had to wear it again the next day. Often we got two to three wears out of it before changing. Then we chose one that had been handed down by a neighbor, or maybe one my sisters had outgrown.

    That was all right though, for it was the way it was! While still living in the shanty, the Peddler came by. I loved when he did. He came during the week on a Thursday. His car was loaded from the trunk to the front seat, leaving him just room enough to drive. He made his stop at each house along Long Branch for the women of the home to get a bill of groceries. I ran with haste on the day he came, to help Mama with her selections. OH, the candy looked so good, but that was off limits. There was only enough money to buy what was needed and nothing more. It was not long until we forgot, for at the next meal we ate a fresh cake or a pie from the items she had bought from the peddler.

CHAPTER 15

We tiptoed out of the bedroom, making sure we made no noise as to wake Mama and Daddy. It was our first endeavor to do something as sneaky or brave as to leave the house while everyone else was asleep. We had to go through the dining room, into the kitchen and out the door before we could set our feet on the porch where we would feel like we were safely on our way. It wasn't very far from the bed to the back door, but I'm such a klutz, if there was anything in our path I'd have managed to kick it, step on it or knock it over. Luckily for us, the moon shown down on the land as bright as day filtering through the trees leaving few shadows but mostly bright moonlight throughout the landscape of the farm. In the country the curtains was of thin fabric, so however they were during the day was how they were after dark. No shades or drapes to close at night, so even through filtered light coming from the window, it was just enough for us to find our way out the door.

It must have been around 10:00 that night as we lay there trying to get to sleep. Why is it when two teens are made to go to bed early, sleep will not come? That's what we did in the country - go to bed early for on the farm morning came too soon. It was a summer night, not hot by any means. During the day in a Tennessee summer, the sun could bring sweat in a new york minute. However when the sun went down in the west, the nights were wonderful.

We had whispered and laughed. The only closet in the house opened into our room. On the other side of the closet was Mama and Daddy's room.

Daddy called out from the other room for us to be quiet and go to sleep. We tried, but our trying only made things worse for we giggled even more and grew wider-awake!

"Whip-poor-will, Whip-poor-will, Whip-poor-will." We stopped talking to listen. The bird seemed to be right on the window sill.

I got up, looked out the window, but didn't see him. Then he sang again, "Whip-poor-will, Whip-poor-will". From this bush to that tree, he sang and sang. We lay there listening to him sing. At times he seemed to get closer to the bedroom window again and sing, and then other times he sounded far away, as though tempting us

.

"Have you ever seen a whippoorwill?" I asked Donna in a hushed voice.

She agreed she had not. Donna was older than I. We shared the little bedroom on the back side of our new house. We were great pals, regardless of the difference in our ages. She was good for me and together we made a pair! I liked her talent. She could draw well, and I liked her stories. I don't remember if she made them up as she went or if she had read them. They were always good. She read a lot and didn't mind sharing her knowledge with me.

In a whisper I said, "I've never seen one either. I wonder what they look like. What color they are".

"Why don't we go outside to see for ourselves?" she whispered.

That did it! All I needed was a nudge anyway. In our night gown, without a house coat, and barefooted, just as quietly as possible - hardly taking a breath in fear of waking someone we started our venture.

The summer night was bright as day with a full moon shining down on the farm, casting shadows that would be eerie any other night.

So here we were on the back porch ready to make a mad dash into the yard. Which direction we were going exactly we hadn't planned; it was according to our little caller. Our only thought was to see the bird. We stood momentarily listening for the night bird. "Whippoorwill" he teased.

We just knew he was on the clothes line in the back yard, but when we got there its call came from a few yards out. We went further talking quietly as we walked. You'd think we would hear his wings flutter as he moved from bush to vine.

It teased us by changing its perch and calling to us again, "Whippoorwill", "Whippoorwill"! We followed his call, moving in another direction, zigzagging across the yard following the singing bird. We just knew we had him this time.

"He's right over there," I whispered. My plan was to slip up on him in the next bush. But the next time he called, he was still further out in the field, and not once did we hear the flapping of his wings.

We walked quietly through the field, giggling and talking low as though someone was listening beside the bird, the dew washing our feet as we went through the grass. One thing was on our mind, and that was to accomplish our mission. We just had to see the bird that sings in the night.

Having never seen a whippoorwill, we could have seen a small blue bird and would not have known the difference. We learned later the whippoorwill got its name by its call. He swoops across the sky hunting insects at night and stops occasionally to announce himself. He is only about 10 inches long. We didn't know what we were looking for, but the venture became an adventure.

Soon we gave up realizing he had out smarted us. Looking back toward the house which was some distance away, we wisely decided that to go any further would mean trouble for sure. The peanut patch was our turning point, for it was on the edge of the bigger field just before going into the woods that bordered the land and separated our farm from the neighbors. We giggled as we walked home, knowing that Mama and Daddy weren't aware we had left the house! It started in an innocent venture to see the night bird, but we felt a little naughty for having slipped out without permission!

CHAPTER 16

Progress caught up with us after a few years of being in the new house. Daddy bought a tractor that would be a big plus for the farm. That Farm-all tractor was the next best thing to a convertible. We begged him to let us drive it. When he drove I stood tall next to him as he made his way through the fields. I was delighted to help him with the harvest.

Getting up early, I mean before sun up on crisp fall days; I managed to wake up after I got to the field I think. We warmed our ungloved hands by the heat from the tractor motor. Gathering corn was a big deal. Daddy got cash for the harvested corn. We spent several evenings around the stove shelling corn from the cob so he could take it to a community called Woolworth and get it ground into meal for the winter. Otherwise the barn held enough to feed the cattle and pigs during the winter with the rest going to market.

I don't know how much help we were. Somehow I managed to make a game out of most things. Still do. So as Daddy took the rows on the left side of the tractor, Dean and I took the down rows, or the ones that the tractor knocked down at the back of the wagon while Donna took the ones on the right.

Donna admits she didn't want to be there. Dean just went along out of obedience, and I was there for I knew I couldn't get away with not going. So Dean and I made a game out of our portion. She was playing basketball on the school team. She was good at playing guard so when she threw the ears of corn, she hit the wagon every time. Me on the other hand - I hurled it kinda wild. Sometimes I hit the basket (wagon) while other times I tossed too hard, it over shot the target but instead it hit Daddy on the head!

"Oh, who did that?" He'd ask as he rubbed his head. Even with a hat on I'm sure it didn't buffer the sting.

"Sorry", I'd say with as little sincerity as I could muster, muffling a giggle.

That didn't stop us. We pulled corn from the stalk and pitched it into the wagon with the flare of a professional basketball player. We played and giggled as we played. I know he was listening to us, but as long as we were getting the job done he said nothing.

"OH, that hurt this time", he yelled as he rose up from his bending position and looked back at us crouching behind the wagon bed.

"Sorry!" I said kind of sheepishly.

With playing and working we finally got through the field and took the wagon load to the barn. Our job didn't stop there. Dean and I climbed the ladder into the loft and shuffled the corn around that he threw in so it would not all be on one side. It was an easy enough task, but dust was everywhere.

The weather kept us from harvesting the corn and tobacco as often as he wanted in order to get the grain in the dry. When our fields were finished, I had forgotten that Daddy had rented other fields where he had planted corn on Long Branch.

Corn was bringing him good money at the market, so he planted more but had to have land. So down to the Busby farm we went early one morning for another cold morning of harvesting the corn; Then on to the Wilson farm a day or two later.

The tobacco he raised was different. I helped in the latter stages of the tobacco crop. He had outside help to cut and tie the tobacco, but not before he had gone out several times in the fall and pulled the suckers form each stalk.

When time came for twisting tobacco, Donna, Dean and I found ourselves in the barn across the creek on the backside of the property. The tobacco leaves had to be twisted, tied with another leaf and laid aside for hanging. Daddy had made the rafters for hanging the tobacco. Then a fire was built. Once the fire was burning strong, it was smothered so that the smoke from the fire would do what it was supposed to do for the tobacco. Smoke it.

We sat cross legged Indian style on the saw

dust ground; Daddy and his daughters. We had conversation but it was not anything meaningful. I believe I probably did most of the talking and the others chimed in, or argued with me. Either way there was talking around the tobacco floor.

Donna said something about Peter Milam, a boy who lived several farms up on Long Branch. He had shown interest in me, or so they said, and to me he was the closest thing to ugly I could think of. He had no form he was so skinny and I'll repeat myself; He was plain ugly.

Their teasing was funny at first, but they continued to rag me until it ceased to be funny. I began taking them serious. I thought they were meaning what they said and I wanted it to stop. None of my insisting would make them stop. So, I gave them one more chance to stop teasing me, or I was going to leave and go home.

They didn't and I did.

Out that barn door, through the field, I made my way home along the well-worn crooked path.. Crossing the creek, through my grandparents yard, to the gravel road and finally into the house where Mama and the younger girls were. I just knew at each turn I would hear Daddy's voice calling me back. Not so.

I got into the house safely when Mama asked, "Through already? Where are the others?"
"They will be here soon", I answered. She didn't ask why I had come sooner than the

others and I didn't volunteer any information. When they arrived home about 30 minutes later I waited for them to chide me for leaving the job before quitting time; I figure I wasn't as important as I thought I was for it never happened!

With supper dishes behind us, we sat down around the living room. Darkness came sooner each night it seemed, but we always had time to sing. Daddy got out the guitar and whatever song came to his mind, he sang. Since we had learned harmony, we joined in and sang with him; a very relaxing time and refreshing our spirit.

CHAPTER 17

As the Shanty was being torn down during the year of 1953, the process of clearing the debris was taking longer than expected. One afternoon as we walked from the bus toward the house, our routine of getting inside and going for a cookie was interrupted. Earlier in the day a fire had been started in a tree stump which had been cut down after the Shanty was torn down, and had decayed enough to burn.

We were so busy talking and planning as we walked. Linda had just started school and was walking with us. Momentarily she took her eyes off the path, pointed at something and called our attention to it as well. None of us were watching where we stepped when Linda fell into the fire and was severely burned. Our screams brought Daddy in from the field and immediately he ran for help. Through the woods behind the house, over fences and up and down hills, he made his way to a cousin's house who owned a car. What seemed like a very long time, he came back in a vehicle driven by Buck Tanner to get Linda and head toward town and the Doctors office.

After getting her to the Dr. who bandaged her little arms and hands, we realized she would be all right. During her recuperating time she had several sisters who fed her, carried her, and nursed her back to health and was glad to do so.

* * *

In 1954 we were old enough to know we were going to have a new baby. As usual we wanted a brother this time, but it was not to be. We were not sent to the O'Guins either; we were allowed to stay home.

Daddy had been working for a nephew doing carpentry work and due to not being paid; they had bought Mama a layette with a bassinet. Times were becoming more modern, and our little Irish town of Erin had a Doctor's clinic, where patients went to see Dr. Atkins instead of him coming to the house to see us. When Mama went into labor, Daddy took her to the clinic to deliver.

Martha was only seven years old, and had been the baby longer than any of us had enjoyed the station in life. When Daddy came home to tell us Mother had another little girl at the Clinic, Martha yelled "I didn't want a baby, I wanted bubblegum". It's a statement we still remind her of.

As was the norm, we looked over the baby girl, Mama named Mary Lois who was born on April 4, 1954. I was soon to be 14 in June when Lois joined the family. Donna was to be 18 in July, and Dean was 15 at the time but would turn 16 in November, whereas Linda would be 10 in July.

Lois was such a novelty as we were old enough to enjoy her. We treated her as though anything she did should have been on the five o'clock news. There wasn't a thing she wanted that we didn't find a way to get. It just so happened what she wanted wasn't something that could be bought, or we'd have been in trouble. There was no money to spend on anything.

Once on a school day, Mama was rocking her. Lois hadn't been feeling well, maybe had a temperature and while Mother was rocking her in a 4 legged kitchen chair (that for sure did not rock) Lois' head went back and she limply lay on Mama's arm. Her eyes rolled back in her head and she quickly turned blue.

Mama began praying. We followed suit. Mama called for the Bible. One of us retrieved it, and Mother immediately laid it on Lois' chest. By then someone had got the attention of the neighbors and Miss Mary Sue Williams came in the door. Immediately she grabbed the Bible off Lois' chest and chided Mother for laying it there. I'm surprised Mama didn't say something back, but the Bible was removed and Lois' eyes came into focus, the bluish color left her body and she began breathing. By then it wasn't necessary to take her to the Doctor. It was discussed with him the next time Mama had to go in.

We could not imagine life without that baby girl; can't even today. In fact we refuse to even consider the possibility.

When I graduated high school Lois was only four and the pride of our life. She posed for our pictures, and was so coddled by her older sisters she never knew not everyone her age was so blessed to have six mothers.

She had always been surrounded by all these "little women" she called her sisters and everything she said was just wonderful to us who listened and watched her every move. Sad as it is, she grew up after I moved away. Both she Linda and Martha became women while I was not watching. And then one day they were my equals.

I lost touch for a few years while I was trying to find my own way. I married in 1960 after graduating high school in 1958. I wasn't ready by any stretch of the imagination to have the responsibility of a family, but perseverance kept us moving hopefully in the right direction.

CHAPTER 18

I think we all came into young womanhood without realizing what was happening to us. Dean did her best to share the facts of life with me from her limited information. As our bodies begin to change so did our emotions and thinking. I'm sure we all wished for a handsome prince to come by and rescue us from the farm. There were plenty of young men at school, but somehow they were not what we were looking for or not interested in us, then too by not participating in very many school activities we didn't get ask out.

In fact one dream we shared was that a plane would crash out in the field. The young pilot would not be hurt, but we would nurse him back to health. He would fall in love with one of use and take us away from the farm to live happily ever after. Not bad day-dreaming I'll have to admit!

Daddy was dead set against us dating anyway. We looked forward to new young people coming to church, or getting to go to fellowship meetings around the district so we could meet other young people. We loved to go on outings down at the Methodist church where other young people were. Just being with the group was good. It was at the Methodist church where I first fell in love. I'm sure Daddy didn't realize I was 17 and by most standards ready to date.

Had I thought about it I'd remembered

Mama was only seventeen when they married. But I was not thinking in terms of marriage, it was good to have someone interested in me. Wait a minute; I'm getting ahead of myself.

Two young men from another county had started coming to church, and ultimately to every community youth gathering any church had. I had met them at the Methodist Church during a youth meeting. They came to the Tennessee Ridge church when I was youth director for our youth service one Sunday night. They were well mannered, well dressed and one of them had a car. Out of the two, one caught my eye. We had talked at each youth event, and I'd get goose bumps when we went our separate ways.

Buck Settles came dressed in a white sport coat and a pink carnation and my heart made flip flops for days just thinking of him.

A country singer by the name of Marty Robbins had the number one hit song that summer. You guessed it, "A White Sport Coat, and a Pink Carnation"! It was when they came to our youth service at another time that Buck asked to take me home. I had been expecting it, so I did the right thing and went to tell Daddy.

"Oh he does, does he?" he said as I smiled and walked away. I had no idea he was against it; his answer was not a no which I would have taken and told Buck I couldn't ride home with him.

I know now I misunderstood his comment, so I got in the car for the short drive home. There were no McDonalds or Wendy's to go to so we went straight home driving slowly and talking as we went. We still got home before the rest so we just stayed in the car and visited some more. Soon headlights from Daddy's car showed into the back window of Buck's car. Daddy didn't stop very far in front of us, when he got out of his car, came to the passenger side where I was setting, opened the door, grabbed me by the arm and told Buck in no uncertain terms to leave and never come back! The humiliation was too much to bear. I grieved because of the embarrassment; I knew Buck hated me; I was so distraught I couldn't eat and eventually I looked hollow eyed and anorexic. Nothing could bring me out of it. I ate enough to keep me alive, but I sure did not need to lose the weight I had lost.

After I graduated in 1958 and went to Nashville to work, I secretly looked for him around every corner and in every store. I grieved for the friendship that might have been. Daddy was afraid it would turn into a marriage and I would not get an education. It may have, but to have the experience of dating at seventeen would have been nice. Today as I write I can truthfully say, he did what Daddy told him to do. He disappeared and I've never seen him since that summer night in 1957.

In our working through the hurt and anger Daddy admitted that he did not realize I was over 17 years old and that he really had no reason to distrust me. I had been saved in a three-week revival two young women had held when I was twelve. I knew I was changed, but no one could explain to me the extent of what had happened inside me; that I was indeed a new creature; Born again, with no past to speak of, only a future. I looked for someone to pattern my life after. I wish now I had had someone to teach me and disciple me; someone to encourage me to read the Bible for my example. Evidently there were good enough examples that I kept going and growing.

My Granddad Chapman saw that I had a Bible with my name on it after I had been saved four years or so. Before that time however my thoughts were on God and I prayed often. On the spring hill by the bluff, or wherever I could find a private place in the house. I'm sure Mama wondered why it took me longer than the rest to go to the spring for water. Many times I prayed in tongues, not knowing that my Spirit was making intercession for me or maybe for others.

I know now they were times of preparation in the prayer closet. I was youth leader at the church. I had nowhere to glean ideas for the youth services. The Spirit of the Lord worked, but so did the enemy. On Sunday night the house was filled with people. At least half were teen-agers. Several who would not go to their own church made it on Sunday night to the youth service at Tenn. Ridge. It must have been the Spirit of a living God that kept them coming, for I know now that I was used mightily and didn't realize it.

I can see Haney Irwin in the congregation; a young man who took his life during those years; unable to face the consequences of some choices he had made. He never did openly make a commitment to Christ, but the Spirit of Love that prevailed must have impacted his life.

Hugh Tanner never made a change that I was aware of. Hugh's brother Barthel died in a tragic car accident a few years later.

Lewis Dennis, Ivon Averitte, Ruby Ferrell; they came and they went. Surely somewhere along the way they heard the message of salvation. Surely I did my part in a small way to share Jesus with them.

During my last years in school, I kept Mama busy. She never knew how many would get off the bus with me in the afternoon. We didn't call them slumber parties; we had a good friendship circle. I do hope I tried to let Mama know in time. She seemed to be prepared with enough food and something extra for dessert. I'm sure Linda, Martha and Lois had to give up their bed for my slumber parties.

Even on Sunday afternoons half the church would come home with us. Mama and Daddy seemed to enjoy the crowd as much as I did. We'd group date, we'd sit around and talk or we'd get a game of baseball going but not before doing the dishes and putting the food away, or before Daddy stopped us from play. I didn't realize it was a "sin" to play ball on Sunday.

The new house many years later built in 1953-54

CHAPTER 19

Eventually Daddy's dreams of his girls getting a high school education came true. From Donna in 1954, Dean in 1956 and me in 1958 Daddy dressed in his only suit and proudly got us there on time to watch as we walked across the stage to receive our diploma.

Mama had made sure we had a new dress to wear under our gown with new shoes. In fact I had gone to Nashville and shopped for mine with Dean's help. I chose a white one with a belted waist that was very complimentary I'm glad to say. I'd never had money to do my own shopping in a store in Nashville no less, so Dean kept me on budget. I think I got to purchase two in fact, as one of them would be for the baccalaureate service on Sunday night before graduation. I loved the feeling of being dressed up - it helped me to hold my head higher than I probably would have normally. It helped thinking I was dressed as well as anyone else and the clothes I wore were not handed down from a neighbor.

I didn't know about GPA's. I only know I had made it through, was a member of the Beta Club, 4-H, choir and things like that. I ordered my records years later and learned I had a 3.7 or 3.9 - and now I don't remember. So I'll just take the last one.......

It just seemed the thing to do for each of us to go to Nashville and find work after graduation. Uncle John Chapman (mama's brother and Aunt Myrtle Chapman (Daddy's sister) had taken us to Nashville many summers for a few weeks to help him in tent revivals. They helped in finding Donna a place to stay until she got established in a job so when Dean graduated she also went. She and Donna got a place together and rode the bus to and from work. I spent a few weeks with them in one of their apartments which was in the most beautiful setting. The grounds were like a park, so well groomed I'd never seen anything quite like it.

That may have been the time when Dean took me shopping, but not sure.

Four years after I graduated Linda followed in 1962. She followed suit and went to Nashville and found work.

Then Martha and Lois who didn't get far from home. As I said in the beginning I don't fault anyone for staying around the home place, for I wish many times I had been that one.

Martha graduated in 1965 and Lois in 1972.

Even though Daddy's dreams had been realized it was Mama who watched us leave and knew things would never been the same again.

Though Daddy, getting older could easily have had thoughts of how things were and were now going to be. But again, he was not the kind to share his feelings to anyone but Mama.

CHAPTER 20

Remembering always makes me melancholy and somber. Time has a way of making us forget all the bad times and hard times and helps us hold only to the good memories. At any time growing up is painful at its best. Cutting the umbilical cord is as hard on Parents as it is the children.

Somehow we know that one day the little ones will leave the nest but to embrace it and accept it when it actually happens we are never prepared for it.

We didn't realize what was going on with Mama and Daddy when the time came too soon, and one at a time for several years in a row there was one less at the table until there was only Lois left. She was only four when I graduated and moved to Nashville. She looked forward to us coming home on the weekend to bring her something. When Donna and Dean moved to Nashville to go to work, I so longed for them to come home and bring me anything. There wasn't much they could bring after buying a bus ticket home. Now and then they'd manage to bring a little something, but the stories they'd tell about their new job and new life was a gift.

Donna eventually went to work for the Nashville Banner in classified advertising, where she would take ads over the phone. It was the policy of the newspaper to assign a different name to the employee taking ads. It was for their privacy and safety. I was so intrigued that her work name was "Doris Day". She was often asked if she was "the" Doris Day.

It was cool to go to Nashville and work for your own money. Seventy-five cents an hour was more than we got as an allowance. There was no money for a 5 cent coke. I made a dollar an hour my first job. I think Dean's first job was in accounting with Hester Batteries. To answer the phone the employees had to answer with, "Start and go with Hester…"

One summer while in the 11th grade, I worked a few weeks for Betty Summers who owned a grocery store and gas station in Tennessee Ridge. I'm sure she found out soon enough I knew very little about what I was doing. I babysat her children after school until she got in from work. So as there was no way to get home, I brought my clothes for a week and stayed after school. I was SO glad to be home on Friday nights. That's where I belonged.

By working there I bought my junior year Album which I cherish today; the only one from my High School years.

I see very well when hindsight is 20/20 and I wish I could have been a better manager.

Maybe I could have brought Martha, Linda and Lois something, for they could not have been much different than me as I anticipated Donna and Dean's visit on the week-end. Had Dean not bailed me out when we lived together in Nashville those two years, I don't know where I'd be. She was so good and patient as her 10 cents an hour seemed to be sufficient to bail me out when my $1. hour wouldn't stretch. She has never complained when it came to helping anyone. I've told her there are some in this world who are blessed with a gift that only God can give them and they use their gift with such ease or afterthought. The Gift of Giving with simplicity. Romans 12.

    I remember vividly when Donna got married. In those days Mama and Daddy never went to our weddings. Donna got married with strangers around her, (her friends instead of her family anyway) but the pictures I've seen of her wedding day with Orra Shelden, she looked very pretty and made a lovely bride.

    Soon they moved away to Washington State. I watched as Mama cried and grieved for her first child who was leaving the nest. She was beginning to see her children taking wings and making a life without her.

    I watched as she eagerly read each letter from Donna. Once Donna didn't have paper to write home on, she wrote on Toilet paper. You talk about eager to hear what she had to say, Mother read it first and we waited with ready ears to hear Mother read it to us.

She somehow read between the lines and felt her daughter was too far away with a man we did not know, even though he was her husband. It is a mother who senses these things concerning her children; a need which has not been expressed, a cry of the heart where no tears are seen. Only a mother.

Sure enough her intuitions were correct. I'm calling it intuitions, but truly it is a God thing. We didn't call it that back then, but only a God who can relate to the heart of a mother, puts these things in her heart. It seems Orra's check got all mixed up and he did not receive one for a while. They had nowhere to turn for food or money. As I understand it, she was pregnant with her first baby girl Connie, and not eating nourishing things was surely not good for her.

It would be at least two years before we would see them again. When they did come we waited with anxious excitement to see them for we would also get to see our first niece.

Connie was the most beautiful blond baby I had ever laid my eyes on. Mama was enthralled with her first grandchild and she wasn't afraid to show it. Connie was the poster child for cerebral palsy in Washington and with braces she had learned to walk by the time she was two. We loved that little girl and her determination to be independent like others her age made us appreciate her more.

CHAPTER 21

Time went by too fast now that I think about it in my frequent visits home. I wish I had paid more attention to life, to the farm, to my family, the sisters, and the land that I sometimes detested.

I wish I had taken time to get to know every detail about each sister, to get inside them and understand what made them tick or kept them going; what their goals and dreams were. I wish I had asked Daddy more questions about himself. I wish he could have been happy.

Maybe he was and again I was too busy in my own growing up world to notice. I wish life could have been better to him. Maybe a son would have helped in making life on the farm easier. I wonder sometimes if I should have been that son.

We've often thought what it would have been like to have had a brother. It is one of those things one can only turn over in the mind and come to any conclusion we want, and make the story end anyway we want to, for it was not to be.

The closest to brothers we could have were our first cousins Donald and Orman. We loved those boys as much as girls would love brothers I'm sure. We were together often, for their father was Daddy's youngest brother and their mother was Mama's best friend. Evonne and Brenda were just more sisters, added to the 6 of us. We always thought Brenda was spoiled, and she probably was for she was the baby in their family. Donald left home to join the Navy when he was 17 but we enjoyed the years we did have and the stories Aunt Nora shared with us.

Orman and I were the same age and even though I was older than Evonne, we never knew there was a difference. We spent Sundays together, and had many family times at their house when they got a TV watching wrestling or a good western.

When we made it home on week-ends, after graduating and moving to Nashville, we did manage to be together as much as we could. We would go to the bluff above the spring and sit with our skirts wrapped around our legs and dream. We had a way of dreaming of our escape from the farm. I really doubt any of us had plans to stay there our entire life - we sure did not dream of the farm getting into our blood stream as it seems to have done.

The world beyond our door was dim. I could hardly visualize borders beyond Tennessee. Studying maps in school was hard to identify with as I could not envision another state or country or oceans. We had relatives that visited us from other states as far away as out west, but to think of ever going west was never in my dreams.

Wondering how their heart could break again or how she could cry another tear, soon another child left home and the pain renewed itself and grew worse until all six were gone. It was then Mama and Daddy looked across the table at each other and realized they were back to where they started 25 or so years earlier. It is a fact of life, or the circle of life we call it. A fact that happens too soon and no one who faces it is sufficiently prepared.

It was my privilege to attend Lois' wedding. Mama and Daddy came and she was so proud they were there. She was beautiful in her white dress and I watched as Mama and Daddy tried to be happy for her. I did not know Daddy's feelings or acceptance of him - I often wondered.

It is sad how we each got married surrounded by strangers. Martha may have had family there as she was still in the country. I look back on the day and realize I made a lot of mistakes, knowing Verlon only a short while, didn't know his family but the church people became my family and they were there to support us. It would have been impossible for Mama and Daddy to have attended a wedding in Mississippi or Alabama, but I've always wished they could have, or I'd have decided to come to Tenn.

With Lois however, it was difficult on all of to know she was traveling across the Atlantic to meet Gary who was already there. She had never been on a plane, but if she was afraid she did not voice it. She braved it alone - well not really alone, she met up with a sweet couple that watched over her most of the way. God was with her I think.

So with the circle of life continuing, it is sobering when we realize that our busy life has been filled to capacity with going and coming, and activity after activity. For Mama and Daddy, I'm glad there was no TV to take our mind off the moments when we were home! I'm glad there was no TV to remind us there was another world outside our little piece of 'land' no one to remind us how poor we were in "things".

Everyone in our community was equal, almost!

We had the land to grow our food, the cows grazed on the rich pastures and gave us milk; the peddler came from town with groceries loading down his car. We'd meet him at the road and look into the back seat, or the trunk and shop for whatever Mama had on her grocery list. Then he'd go on to the neighbor's house.

We were equal even if our neighbor went to their church and we'd go to ours. Even then there was a distinct difference, though no one could explain it to our satisfaction. We visited their church. They never visited ours. When we did visit theirs, they'd ask Mama to pray. I was always so proud of her. She was bold!

Mama took the evangelist in. She made them comfortable. She'd invite the pastor and his family to stay with us Sunday afternoons. We had no parsonage for him to live in, so he'd drive from Clarksville 30 miles away. There was always enough food and while she and the pastor and his wife went over church books or visited, we entertained their children. Mama's house was refuge for them, a place to rest for a few hours. She shared our clothes with the evangelist wife. Didn't matter we were close to being naked ourselves, we had enough to share was her philosophy.

Those were happy times, precious times and a good beginning for us all. For that it all the first 17 years or so are – just a beginning – a start for us to take what we have learned and add to it; making a life of our own on the basis of that beginning. Destiny has a way of slipping up on us I've decided. Very few people in life actually get what they aim for. Maybe their aim is off target. Maybe their dreams were fuzzy and never verbalized never coming into focus because it was never really clear what the dream was.

Many of us accept what comes to us, never realizing that God has always had a plan and wants us to seek Him so that He can show us the plan that will fulfill our lives. Often it takes us years to realize we may have missed the course, but God in all His mercy helps us get back on track.

I am blessed. To have had both parents in my aging years when even my nest was empty, is truly a blessing. My heart yearned to care for them and make their lives easier.

I don't like "old age" I've decided. It is cruel. Daddy was ready to live for a long long time, but his bones were saying slow down. He'd grasp and work at keeping his mind sharp so that he could stay independent. He read and kept up with the news and goings on in the world.

CHAPTER 22
MAMA

Mama's health began failing in the late 80's. Each time I went home she wanted to talk about different things in her life. I listened and tried to offer encouragement. I prayed with her to forgive those who had held her in bondage through hurts in her life.

She started sleeping in the spare bedroom with her radio close by listening to Gospel music. Some she had recorded so she could play again and again. I'm grateful to whoever got her the tape player recorder for it was a God send while she was "cleaning her slate" as I called it.

She wrote each of us a letter to be opened after death. She wrote her last wishes for us to know what she wanted for her funeral.

Often I gave her a bath. Home health nurses came but I believe it was later as her health deteriorated. I combed her hair - she talked some more about what she wanted. I tried to encourage her we would carry out her wishes the best we could.

Eventually she started repeating herself. She told the same things over and over and we politely listened and tried to be understanding. She told the same jokes we had heard in childhood again and again.

She recalled her miscarriages and remembered they were all boys. I'm not sure she took time to grieve the babies at the time, as life had called her back to activity soon after she was able to get up and go again. However when she told us she had not named them, it was important for her to let us know she had named them. When she got to heaven, she would want them to know she had given them a name. So the baby boys became real again after she had given them names.

It was through no fault of his own that Daddy had come to the end of his expertise and realized through much anguish he could not give her the care she needed.

"I promised God I would take care of her the rest of her life and I can't do that if she is in a nursing home." As it was they had been together for 60 years and felt he was going back on a promise to God if he quit now.

After much grief of soul, the Doctor's worked with Daddy and signed the papers to place her in the Waverly Nursing home. It was the beginning of the end. We knew it was.

About a year after she had become a resident in the nursing home, I felt a strong need to go home. I was uncomfortable driving myself that long distance for some reason, so I asked a dear friend if she would go with me. May the Lord bless Peggy Brown for gladly going home with me that overnight trip and patiently wait for me to visit Mama. I sang to her, we giggled about anything and nothing. I lay down beside her in the bed and we talked some more. We remembered the time when Verlon and I went home and she and I would sleep together in the room upstairs so we could talk. Well, it was more her talking than me. I was so tired I would listen as long as I could, and drift off to sleep in mid-sentence. We laughed and called it our slumber party. Come morning she would make her way back down the steps and start breakfast. I declare she would rattle pots and pans until I got up.

"I declare, you could call me and I'd have got up. You didn't have to make so much noise". We'd have another chuckle and start our day mostly filled with nothing but being together. It was a time I don't remember ever experiencing before and now I realize it was a special time God gave me to hold on to.

There was a time when her six girls took her on a week-end to Paris Landing state park. That was the most special gift any of us could have given her. She was like a little girl, and really did not know how to express her gratitude for being a part of the special time with just her and the grown women she called her girls. I believe it was one of the highlights of her last years, I'm so glad we were able to do with her.

More about Daddy
When Mama went into the nursing home, he

cried. "I promised God 60 years ago I would take care of her until death separated us." It was difficult to see him so distraught when he realized he could no longer do "his" job. He was strong however and eventually he realized the best decision was letting her go.

Looking back he didn't stop caring for her; because daily he made visits to the Nursing home. Her need for care was much more than he was able to do. His skills were limited to preparing her meals and doing a load of wash and administering her meds. Her care was the first and foremost thing on his mind and with prayer and encouragement from his children did the only thing he could do.

So on those daily visits, he parked the car, carefully reaching beside him to retrieve the "fried pie" wrapped in paper he had prepared for her. After kissing her, he gave her the pie and her words were usually "Thank you daddy, lay it there, I'll it in a little while".

It was difficult to visit her and hear her cry to go home. We did taker her home occasionally, and at first she cried not to be taken back. Eventually though as her sickness progressed her cries were turned around. The next time she would beg to go home - and we knew this wasn't home anymore.

CHAPTER 23

Some days my heart cries as I remember Mama, I miss her so.

♦ The independent lady who kept her house spotless and cooked meals that you dreamed of going home to.

♦ The ingenious lady who could issue orders like a sergeant and make memories with us while she involved us in her Saturday house cleanings.

♦ The mostly shy lady that loved the Lord in her own way. She was gifted with what the Bible calls the "gift of hospitality".

♦ A lady with a heritage of Godly parents whose influence still lives on in their grand and great grandchildren and more generations. The story is passed down that her Mother, Grand Mama Chapman prayed for the Lord to raise up ministers in her family. The prayer is still being answered today.

♦ I find myself wishing I could have taken the pain of loneliness away from Mama; wanting to pick up the phone, calling her house and hearing her answer. Wanting to hear her tired jokes once again and hear her ask how are the "kids"?

♦ "What are they doing now?"
♦ How is Greg and Debbie?
♦ "Is Janean and Sandy married yet?"
♦ What about Tom is he still playing ball?
♦ "Have you heard from Verlon and

when will he be home?"

Most often her last words would be, "Hurry home, it gets awfully lonesome sometimes without you girls!"

I can still visualize her only months before she fell and broke her hip, standing on a chair, with a dust cloth in her hand trying to get a cob web down from the ceiling fan or from a far corner. A short time later she broke the other hip, and then an arm. It was the beginning of the end, and I am still emotional at the thought.

Standing on a chair is a thing of the past for her, but my mental vision of her standing there is still real. I wasn't ready for her to get old. I wasn't ready for her to leave us.

I know that is not realistic. It is the circle of life. We are born and eventually we die. And somewhere in between we live. Being close to the age when she left us, makes me to know life is short and brief. Daddy said the same thing with living past 100. Life was too short.

At my age, my life needs to go smoother, and does when everything around me stays the same! That isn't realistic thinking either. I always come around to the changes, but it does take a while.

I once tried to visualize life without them; Mama and Daddy. I realized it was inevitable, so I tried to savor the moments of every visit.

I knew the day would come when the six of would go home to the Reunion and someone would be missing. It could be a precious sister. Most likely it would be our parents who were the reason for the get-to-gather in the first place.

I visualize the 6 of us walking around the bluff and spring and trying to reminisce about our yesterdays. The elements and time have changed the looks of our path and our dreaming place on the bluff.

Nothing stops us though. We take a walk around the bluff anyway, and remember our dreams that reached into an unknown world outside our haven. Regardless of how the spring is trying to dry up, and the landscape has changed, and the milk house is no more, we will surely remember the cold spring water as it came from under the bluff; we'll remember the cool drink of water which was so refreshing on a hot summer day.

We try to find the path back up the hill. Somehow the hill up to the road seems shorter and the path is no longer visible.

We look out across the field and visualize tall corn stalks ready to be harvested.

We may even go wading in the creek, remembering the "foot-log" that served as our bridge to the path that led to O'Guins farm.

We may silently remember the cattle that grazed in the field on O'Guins farm. Our path then followed the edge of the field, and we'd pray the cows stayed on the other side or in the middle and did not venture toward us as we walked. Now the cattle are gone and there is no need to fear.

We may recall going to Grandma Lil O'Guin's house and have Hennon open the door with that famous smile covering her face as she welcomed us in and usually had a treat for us. Good memories of those two precious ladies who always loved us the way we were and accepted us the same.

We may even remember the spring floods that came fast and furious, and caused the rock creek to overflow its banks and threaten to get into Grandma and Grandpa's house. We may talk about the good swimming hole the deluge left.

We may talk about Aunt Nora's Chocolate Pie she made just for us.

We sometimes will talk about Grandpa Tanner and his Sun dial clock. He had made marks on the old wooden porch and when the sun caused a shadow to get to a certain mark, he knew it was 2:00 in the afternoon, or to another mark, it was later, and so on. I was intrigued! It worked for him at least. It was an invention that he gladly shared with little ears and curious eyes, but try as I might I could not tell the time when he wasn't there to explain again!

"Do you remember the old gentlemen that lived on Waverly Road going into Erin, that would come get us to take us to singings?" I'll probably say. "Once we spent the night at their house. I couldn't have done it if you girls had not been there with me. I was so afraid and if I remember correctly he smelled bad!"

"Was he married? Surely he was, or Daddy would not have let us go anywhere with him." I'll continue. "He was a good man to take us places. I enjoyed the singing at different churches. Wish I hadn't been so shy then to have talked in between songs. Don't guess it mattered though!"

(PS) You all may have been glad I didn't!!

Occasionally we will recall with tears and sadness the tobacco crop that went up in smoke as the rented barn burned down. There was no insurance and a season of hard work and labor had been lost in a matter of minutes. It was always difficult to hear Daddy cry, much less watch him.

And even though I had already moved away from home, my heart broke with empathy remembering the time consuming work involved in the process of getting the tobacco to the barn, twisting it for hanging, and then for its final curing before taking it to the market. He became a broken man for a long time, broken to the extent of despondency. He gave up ever raising another crop of tobacco.

We may walk down the road to "Brown's Store" that is no longer there. Just to see if it is 5 miles we thought, or more like 1/2 mile! We'll reminisce about Miss Alice and her wonderful hospitality and how she made each of us feel special even if we didn't have a nickel to spend. I'll remember always how she let me play the piano to my heart's content.

We'll laugh when we remember "dollar" Brown.

We may dream of driving the tractor, and pretending we're just learning to drive and it is a Corvette convertible instead of a Farm-all tractor.

Maybe our children will walk with us and take part in our history and try somehow to be a part of the story. Maybe not. For after hearing of Mama's stories I'm sure I never walked with her around the old home place where her memories were embedded. As for Daddy's memories, he shared them as long as he thought he had our attention or when took time to stop long enough and listen.

Life is balanced I've decided with good times and not so good times. But occasionally, life seems to hand us times I've labeled as "the night times of the soul".

- Times when hope seems out of our reach.
- Times when the days are long and nights even longer and morning seems days away.
- Circumstances too big and decisions have to wait.
- Times when the heavens are brass and God seems to be busy elsewhere.
- Times when the Doctor says, you have cancer.
- Times when you hear the words of "an incurable blood disorder."
- The first time you hear the word "Dementia" when the Doctor is talking about your husband.
- Or the loss of a husband seems unbearable and time spent together was just too short.
- When the D word is spoken and before one knows it the Judge says your marriage is over.
- How does one pick up after realizing the love that brought us together is no more?
- When there is too much month left over at the end of your money.
- Night times - night times of the soul when it seems there will never be light shining again on a better tomorrow. Somewhere in our life we experience at least one of these or definitely one by another name.

Night times of the soul! When life deals this hand, I want to be still. Maybe in being still in my spirit, God will allow me to hear the call of the night bird somewhere in the distance to remind me that God is still the same even in the night, for he made both.

I'll know too He is still the God of my childhood, the same now as He was back in the 50's. He never changes; He doesn't hide. I'm the one who has "lost" Him momentarily and the night time will pass. "Be still" the bible says. "Be still and know that I AM GOD!" Psalms 46:10

The Whippoorwill sound takes me back to a time of no worries no cares, for someone else was in charge of seeing to my needs.

Upon hearing his call, I'll feel the urge in me to run immediately to the farm. I'll probably sit out under the stars and sing again. I'll sing the familiar songs that have made their mark on my soul for eternity and maybe the Whippoorwill will sing harmony with me again. He and I will lift our voices and the darkness will seem as nothing as the music rises from my soul once again.

My song will return, the sun will shine again and the darkness that crowded my soul for a moment, as it sometimes does, will dissipate all because of the **Whippoorwill's song** that takes me back.

Doris 2014 -
With much love.

The Whippoorwill

Final Note:

To say this is all there is - I can't. It has taken several years to write what I've written. I'm sure there will be a time when I will "wish I'd have written that too." Especially when I hear your input and a memory you have that differs from mine.

That is OK because, again these are my memories. Please accept them as such for my sake, write your own memories down and pass them on to me. You know I've made up some things, based on some of my thinking over the years as a woman. Who knew what went on in their quiet time, other than her tears she shared with us. But conversation, I've used my imagination as to how they thought or felt, I again have "filled in the blanks."

Love you girls desperately, and all the extended family whom you allow to read this. We have a legacy and I want to pass it on.

>Doris
>2014

Similar to our Shanty on the front side.

The Shanty

A string of fresh fish

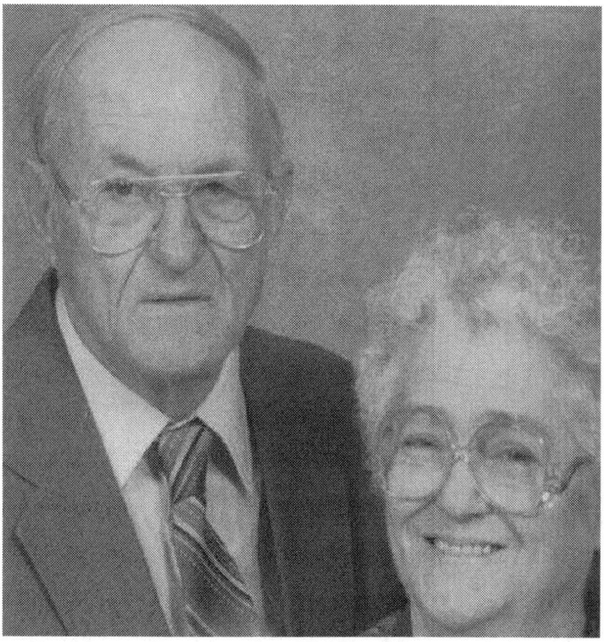

Mama's Girls

The New House built in 1952-53

The following stories are taken from my website at Writing.com. I've chosen the ones that I had the most hits on, and the most comments.

If you enjoy them, fine, but if not I at least have them in a bound book for me to keep.

Thanks again,
Doris

Miss Alice

"Miss" Alice is what we called her. In fact we addressed our teachers as "Miss". Didn't matter if they were married with children, we addressed them as Miss.

Miss Alice wasn't a teacher (at school anyway), but that's what we called her. Miss Alice had a last name, but that doesn't really add to her story. We didn't think of her as being anyone's mother, or anyone's wife. She was just Miss Alice, one of the most genuinely kind people I have ever encountered; a lady who made an impression on me for all time, as a little girl growing up on Long Branch.

She and her family had moved from the North to settle in our community. The house they bought was a plantation house of sorts, which I had never noticed before she moved there. In going to and from church and school I had to have passed it on a daily or weekly basis, but it never had significance before. It was on a hill and to me it stood tall in all of its two story glory.

She and her husband built and operated a small grocery store with a gas pump. That was wonderful for I had never lived in walking distance of a store. Having the money to purchase a piece of candy was a treat, even if it didn't happen very often.

It was Miss Alice who nurtured in me my desire to play the piano. She had one. She was the musician at her church, and to hear her play the hymns just by reading the notes was so awesome to me. I think she must have loved playing for inevitably she did me a mini concert of sorts each time I found an excuse to go to her house. She saw my thirst to learn, so she began giving me lessons. Nothing major, but enough to feed my hunger to touch the piano like I knew what I was doing. We didn't have a piano. A guitar was the instrument at our house, but I felt like I had a piano when she gave me permission to "play".

A dear lady whose name I do not remember game me piano lessons at school. I'd have her play it for me, and I would play what I heard reading very few notes. I borrowed a beautiful formal from a friend and was able to go to the piano recital at the end of the school. I know there is a picture of me somewhere but it didn't wind up with me. Anyway...

I left the farm life on Long Branch when I graduated from High School. Employment, more education and family kept me away from the area for the most part. I did see Miss Alice on occasion when I visited home. Mama filled me in with the answers to my questions concerning her. She gave me updates when I'd ask; about Miss Alice's boys going to college, and moving back up north, or about her losing a brother in death, or about her husband who took ill.

When I did settle down to see her, it was an accident. An accident, in that, it was a pleasant surprise to know she was close by. "Miss Alice is down the hall," Mother said while we visited.

"Oh Really!" I responded gladly. It is amazing how situations work outside our little box of a mind, to bring the jig saw puzzles pieces together. Mother's health had deteriorated to the extent that she needed constant care and the Nursing Home was the most likely choice.

The nursing home was in the town of the countryside where we grew up. For the most part I guess it was nice, but as far as nursing homes go it was still a place of aging citizens who were never expected to get well again. The staff tried to keep them comfortable and wait for their bed to be empty so they could place another aging soul in their place.

Miss Alice husband had died leaving her alone in that big ole house. With her boys living out of State they were faced with a big decision.. After selling the farm, they too were forced to make the choice of giving their mother constant care which they were not able to give. I had heard she had Alzheimer's but was not prepared for what occupied the room down the hall.

I walked outside of Mama's room into the hall; Hesitating for a moment to think through my first response to her before I moved on.

The hopes I had of a jovial meeting with my longtime friend, died when I saw an old woman come out of the room. Surely it couldn't be Miss Alice.

"Maybe it was her roommate" I thought more in a wish. I didn't recognize this woman. I figured I must have misunderstood Mama's directions. So I walked back and asked again.

"Someone told me she was in room 210 down the hall." Mama repeated. I didn't take time to tell her why I asked a second time.

Sure enough the woman I saw was only a shell of where the Miss Alice I knew once lived. Alzheimer's had taken her mind and ravaged her body. She never looked up as we passed in the hall. With her head down, she mumbled unintelligible words and kept shuffling on down the hall. I'm glad my memory of her was imbedded in the eyes of that pre-teen that walked the mile down the road. Picking up pace as I got closer to her house, I would slope up the hill, ring the doorbell only to have Miss Alice welcome me as if I was a long lost relative, or an important celebrity.

Shortly after we passed in the hallway she disappeared into the dining/fellowship room down the hall out of sight. I stood and watched her go, knowing there was nothing I could say she would understand.

However for a moment I was back in her living room listening to her play the piano. She had found the piano in the dining room and set down to play. It was still a hymn. It wasn't perfect, but it was beautiful just knowing that her love for the piano was still inside that shell. What I heard helped my memory of yesterday to stay alive. I don't dwell on what the disease had done to her. I like the version the little girl inside me recalls most often when I set down at the piano and play a hymn.

July 2006
Doris Thompson

© **Copyri**ght 2006 Doris (UN: datanner at Writing.Com). All rights reserved.
Doris has granted Writing.Com, its affiliates and syndicates non-exclusive rights to display this work.

THE SILENCE

"I sit here some days and never say a word," he said with a faraway look in his eye. I wanted him to continue.

"Really?"

"Yea, maybe for days at a time I never hear my own voice."

It was difficult for me to listen as I knew what he was saying. I had been concerned about him being alone. He lived in the same house where he and his childhood sweetheart Sarah had raised their family. Mama had died seven years earlier, and he had remained in the house with all the memories. Pictures of my sisters and me, and our children were still in place where she had hung them, or placed them on a shelf. The chair where she had spent her last days before going to the nursing home was still part of the living room where he stayed. The chest of drawers in the spare bedroom still had her personal items forever reminding us that she had lived there. Remembering Mama and her last years of struggle, didn't dampen the feeling of being close to her when I laid down on the bed or touched her clothes still hanging in the closet. She was there in each curtain, or picture on the wall, or seemingly around each corner.

Daddy moved from the breakfast table to the porch. He walked with the aid of a three legged cane. Steps not as sure as they once were. He adjusted his chair so his face and body would be toward the sun. "I have to bake my knees in the sun, so they won't hurt so bad." he said, as he settled into his chair.

His hearing aids whistled, but he did not notice.

"You know? Not many people my age can say they was successful." He said, as he shifted his body getting comfortable. I set behind him in the porch swing, longing to see his face as we talked.

"I know Daddy" I replied.

"I was a success at anything I done," he said. "The farm, you girls. All of you got a good high school education and got an office job. Didn't have to work in the field like you did when you was kids."

I had to add, "None of us ever gave you any problem or heartache. That really is success in its truest sense!"

He heard me, but never responded. He raised his eyes to look out over the farm. The fields where his cattle once grazed belonged to someone else now.

I got up to stand beside him. "I remember the hog pen down yonder", I said as I pointed to the spot hoping to engage him further, He had had the good sense to make the pen away from the house on a rise above the creek.

"We had them named," I ventured. "One we named Arnold!" Again, he didn't respond. I too was lost in my own thoughts. It was always difficult to learn which hog would be butchered come winter. By the time we put the fried tenderloin and biscuit in our mouth, we had forgotten that it once had a name.

Now and then he nodded understandingly, but he had thoughts of his own. I kept listening. At times he talked as though talking to himself. I think he was listening to a human voice even if it was his, or could it be these were the thoughts he had when he was alone and now with someone to listen he was ready to share?

"We had corn in that field, didn't we? Maybe tobacco in that bottom land across the creek." I asked just to keep him talking. I was thinking of how difficult it must have been on a farmer to have 6 daughters and no sons.

The land had changed over the past 50 years and what we saw in our memory was all we had. Today we saw mobile homes, drive ways and automobiles that spotted the scenery where stalks, heavy with corn once stood tall.

The creek had changed its course. Years and the elements had made the once rolling water a little more than a stream. Only memories remain of the swimming hole where we went on summer days to get cool. (Mama told us not to get in too deep water until we learn to swim!)

We watched as Daddy came home from the creek, with a string of fish, knowing we would get to eat of his bounty.

The story of the farm was always interesting to us as adults. We loved getting him to talk about how he had it paid for in a year or two. How he bought more acreage from the neighbor as he could. One hundred dollars an acre some for less. There was a pride about owning and farming your own land. His dad had never owned property. He had just share cropped other's land.

He talked about the team of mules that pulled the plow through the dirt to make furrows where seed would be dropped. How one of them once kicked him and broke a rib. He talked about clearing new ground and killing a rattle snake or a copper head. His memory was vivid and I listened, even though I had heard some of the stories before.

"I never will forget the first tractor I bought. It sure was better on my legs since I didn't have to follow behind the team."

"It was red wasn't it"? I interrupted.

"No, it was green" he corrected me.

Red, Green. I just knew that tractor was the nearest thing to an automobile we had at the time, and setting high on the tractor, I'd pretend it was a convertible. Otherwise the wagon, pulled by the team of mules, was our transportation to and from my Uncle's house or to church on Sunday.

He remembers that I was new at driving but I pestered him until he allowed me to drive the tractor forward in the field. We had been helping him (and I use the words lightly) gathering corn. Once we had cleaned the stalks around us, it was time to move forward, so he would get on the tractor and pull the wagon several lengths ahead. However, he finally gave in to "let me do it this time". Somehow, I turned the wheel too deep and I headed for him. He was yelling and instructing me to "turn it the other way". I turned the wheel the other way, but again I turned too far, and started for him again. I panicked, but finally stopped the tractor, and was not allowed on it again, until I had better instruction.

He moved to another subject. "This community has changed so much since we moved here 65 years ago. I don't even know nobody any more. All the neighbors that lived here then have gone on. I don't know nobody in these parts," he continued.

I silently agreed, for I was remembering a few widows who lived down the road still, but could not remember any men of his era. When you are 98 you outlive your neighbors and even your children in some cases.

He talked about his first job, his first automobile. He recalled the first time he had his picture made.

"I was 18. Would you believe it took me that long to see myself in a picture?"

We still have the picture. He looked sharp. Three piece suit, a hat and tie. Sharp for an aging teenager! Made on the streets of Detroit. His brother was also in the picture. His brother is still living, and his children have the same picture. Our Fathers in their late 90's was once 18! It was so difficult to visualize, we needed a picture to remind us they had had a life before us!

As much as I dreaded leaving the picture of him baking himself in the sun, reliving his yester years, and the conversation that ensued, I knew we needed to start the long trip back to Arkansas. For sure this was one of those days I didn't want to go. My husband had packed the car as I lingered on the porch, taking a few more precious minutes to implant the vision of him on my memory for all times, never knowing whether we would have a conversation like this again. One is on borrowed time when one reaches 98+, and too, I knew he would be left alone to listen to the deafening silence.

"Daddy we need to start home", I told him.

"You coming back for the gathering?" he wanted to know. That meant the family reunion in a couple months.

"Oh yes, we'll be here" I assured him.

I knew when we were gone that his eyes would follow us until we were out of sight. I knew also that he would watch the mail for a letter from "the girls". I knew he would wait patiently for the phone to ring around 10:30 in the morning when his baby girl would make her daily call to check on him. I also knew he would eat a light lunch, so he would be ready when Martha came in later in the day to bring a hot supper.

In the meantime, wrapping his arthritic fingers around the neck of an out of tune guitar, he would sing, to what would look and feel like, an empty room. He might turn the CD player on and listen to a good ole blue grass gospel song that reminds him of Heaven and home where Sarah is waiting. But mostly he will listen to the Silence.

Written after a visit home in April, 2006
Doris Thompson
© Copyright 2006 ark mom (UN: datanner at Writing.Com). All rights reserved.

© Copyright 2006 Doris (UN: datanner at Writing.Com). All rights reserved.
Doris has granted Writing.Com, its affiliates and syndicates non-exclusive rights to display this work.

It was not my Intention to Snoop

By Doris Thompson

It isn't like me at all to rummage in someone's dresser or closet. It is totally out of character, and I am appalled at anyone who does. I have taught my children that, as curious as they may be, being nosy and looking into someone's cabinet or drawers was a no, no.

They did manage to get themselves locked in a bathroom or two. I don't think it was to see if other people kept anything in their cabinets different than we had at home. I've decided that four, five, and six-year-olds have a natural tendency to explore. They had to try everyone's bathroom, like it was gonna' be different than the one at home. I never knew if they rummaged where they had no business. No one ever complained anyway. For sure neither of them ever told me if the other one snooped.

So why would I break my own stern rule? Again, it is totally out of character for me.

In February of 1999, Mother died, and it was after that, I found myself going through the dresser and chest of drawers in her home. My sisters and I had made a pact to leave things as she had left them. Daddy needed consistency at this point in his life and we were thinking of him. Walking into her house even a month or two after she was gone, we found things, as they were when she was there. I almost expected to find her in the kitchen or taking an afternoon nap in the spare bedroom. However with no cooking aroma coming from the kitchen it was obvious that things weren't the same. I knew she would not show up at the door or answer me had I called out to her.

My husband and I settled in. We unloaded the car, ate supper, watched a program on TV, and visited with Daddy. I got up momentarily to turn the covers down on the spare bed where we would sleep. Naturally the smell and spirit of Mama was in the room. Her house slippers were on the floor next to the closet door. Her robe hung in the closet along with the cotton dresses she wore after the home health nurses gave her a bath. The suit dresses she wore when she was able to go to Church were also visible.

I turned to the chest of drawers and opened the top drawer. I wasn't thinking about it being not in my personality or make up to search where I had no business.

However, it was mama's house and I wasn't going to take anything. I seemed to be driven with a desire to find something - anything that would bring her back to me. Her socks were marked with S. Tanner in black ink. Several pairs in fact. It was evident this was the drawer in which my sisters had placed her belongings from the nursing home. I needed a pair to wear with my tennis shoes the next day, so I laid a pair on the bed.

From there I moved to another drawer. Her toiletries-bath powder, lotions, deodorant, cologne and fragrant soap all lay neatly in their places. I stood momentarily breathing in the smells that were so familiar. I picked up the bottle of cologne and held it to my nose. Why was I so driven with the need to see her or touch her or something that belonged to her?

It was getting late, so we each said our good night salutations, and went to bed. The raised window allowed the sound of crickets, whippoorwills, and bullfrogs into the room. The fan hanging from the ceiling whirled a quiet roar that lulled us to sleep as we closed our eyes and sank into the soft mattress.

The brightness of the morning came too soon. The room was on the east side of the house and the sun came looking for us as it rose above the budding trees. I rose early thinking of Daddy. He always looked forward to my home made biscuits. It was a treat for me to prepare breakfast in Mama's kitchen. My breakfast didn't taste like Mama's cooking I'm sure, but I had learned from the best and enjoyed trying.

After the dishes were put away, I got dressed for the day, donning my borrowed socks with the black letters "S. Tanner" I felt complete. We had planned the day with Daddy - maybe a ride around the community - go to the gravesite and "visit" with Mama. But that would have to wait. I lingered in the bedroom.

The urge was there again. I did not have second thoughts about opening another drawer in the dresser. This one was filled with sheets, pillow cases-some never used, others showed their age. All were neatly folded.

The next one had her underwear and her half and full slips that no respected woman would be without. They were folded, waiting for someone, anyone to select one to wear. More sheets to fit both twin and full-size beds. I wondered if she had forgotten how many she had.

I gave up - finding nothing in particular and went on my way. A weekend is a short time to go home and expect to do much. We always relish the time we have with Daddy, but Sunday comes and the trip home is always before us. We promised to return as soon as we could, and immediately started planning another trip a few months later. On returning my home I had no further thoughts about my poking around in what would otherwise be places of privacy.

It took me several trips back home to find what I must have been looking for. I don't think I have ever had such a driving urge to finish a task as I did then, and even worse, I could not explain it to my Sisters or husband..

I did not think about it being something Mama wanted me to do. I just figured with my dime store psychology that I must have been looking for Mama in some weird way.

On each visit, it was as though something or someone was drawing me into the bed room. I gently and thoroughly kept looking and probing in each drawer. Each drawer led me to another, and to another until each one was examined.

What I found however, was not in a dresser, chest or china cabinet drawer. On one of my earlier scavenger hunts, I had noticed a basket that sat beside the chest. It was on the floor behind the door. To me it just appeared to be "stuff", as Mama was known for keeping things that were of no value to anyone but her. Some papers, folders, writing pads, note cards and such were in no special order.

The day came when I sat down on the made-up bed and gazed around the room slowly telling myself to give up. However, the basket with all her "stuff" caught my eye. Thoughtfully I picked it up and sifted through a few of the things. A folder captured my attention. The basket didn't seem important anymore. Inside the folder were six sealed envelopes. On each envelope in Mama's hand writing, was the name of each of her girls. I naturally found the one addressed to me and held it close.

As Mama's health began to decline she slowly accepted her ultimate death several years before she died. Age, a bad heart, and diabetes were slowly taking her away from us. She recognized the end was eminent. Neither I nor any of my sisters wanted to accept the idea that she would soon be leaving us. She tried talking to us about her last wishes but it was difficult to hear. I'm sure in our inability to respond to her, we led her to believe we weren't listening to her. She was working on unresolved issues that had plagued her. Some things we knew, but they weren't as important to us as they were to her. She was doing a cleansing of sorts that everyone must face in time.

On one visit, she might be a little girl again in the playhouse with her corn shuck dolls. The next visit she may be the young bride, just married and leaving her Mother and Daddy with her new husband. Even yet, on another visit she would talk about each new baby and how difficult her pregnancies had been, or how small the baby was. For sure she wanted to talk about the three little boys she had miscarried. Life had been hard but she had happy memories that overrode them most of the time. She was proud of her daughter's accomplishments. She loved the day the phone rang and one of them would be on the other end of the line. "Just checking on you today," one of us would say, and then we would give her an opportunity to tell us whom she had seen, whom she had talked with on the phone, or what the Doctor had said.

Then somewhere in between the phone calls, or maybe during the wee hours of the morning when she was unable to sleep, she started writing these letters. It appeared she spent time writing down on paper what she wanted us to know, but wasn't sure we had heard. I wonder how long it took her to write each one.

The envelopes were sealed. Each message was

private. If we wanted to share with each other, we could. Otherwise it became one more word from Mama, but this time from the grave. Her messages reassured us that she loved us, and was proud of us, and would hopefully see us in the next life. My yen to search the room stopped that day. The message I received, I might have missed had I not broken my own rule.

© Copyright 2006 Doris (UN: datanner at Writing.Com). All rights reserved.
Doris has granted Writing.Com, its affiliates and syndicates non-exclusive rights to display this work.

Made in the USA
Charleston, SC
20 April 2016